THE RUSSIA WE FACE NOW

By

ETHAN T. COLTON

(Author: The X Y Z of Communism and
Four Patterns of Revolution)

AND OTHERS

THE PUBLIC AFFAIRS INSTITUTE

312 Pennsylvania Avenue S.E. • Washington 3, D. C.

INTRODUCTION

The Public Affairs Institute takes pleasure in publishing this book on the important subject of the Russia we face. In doing so the Institute believes the material represents a high level of scholarship.

Dr. Ethan T. Colton and his collaborators have brought to this presentation a wealth of knowledge and experience. Their insights should materially aid busy readers to understand the current proposals and counterproposals concerning our foreign relations vis-a-vis the Soviet government. Their unswerving allegiance to our Democracy and the free world make their seasoned interpretations of special value to all who seek to promote peace based on a realistic appraisal of the Soviet threat.

The Public Affairs Institute is a nonpartisan, nonprofit, research foundation seeking to promote wider public knowledge and appreciation of current problems. In choosing a competent person to conduct the research, making available the facilities of the Institute to aid in the research, and finally in publishing the results, the Institute has discharged its obligation. It does not take responsibility for the facts or findings, that being the function of the author and his associates.

DEWEY ANDERSON
Executive Director

CONTENTS

FOREWORD

Over the past decade Joseph Stalin exercised a profound influence among rulers. His relinquishment of that power in death flashed two compelling first questions across the world. "Who and what next?"

Meshes of speculation have been woven around the anxious inquiry by the reportorial, columnist and editorial galaxy of writers. Early events have already shown most of these guesses and wishes to be lacking the substance of realism.

Eager, impatient watching goes on for action from the Kremlin of a character that is bound to prove heavy with the fate of mankind. Is Malenkov the actual Kremlin chief, or only a "first among equals"? In either case what are the qualities and abilities of this hitherto little publicized figure? Will or can Mao act independently? Have prospects increased of satellite eruptions occurring in some quarter of the revolutionary fatherland?

How about a rise or lowering of "cold war" temperatures? If it suits the purposes of the new Moscow administration, there may be a period of "peaceful penetration" instituted. One of the "intervals" may be upon us— perhaps a major, indulged before when a relaxation of aggression has better served the party ends. If on balance the party chiefs conclude that they have obtained as much as is possible now out of a "hot war" in Korea or elsewhere, the tactic may shift to another in the Communist repertoire. The new approaches may range widely from Asia to the UN headquarters in the United States, to Berlin in the heartland of Europe. They may look very much like the "real thing," forerunners of the world peace all of us long for so deeply. And we will be well advised to take every advantage of any offering which improves the real chances for peace, which moves us forward to the attainment of our democratic goals. Likewise, most careful re-examination of the body of enduring fact accumulated since the Communists took power in 1917, will be the essence of timely wisdom to gauge from it what may be expected to emerge as post-Stalin practices. It is this long-established body of fact which forms the basis of our study of the Russia we face now.

The Communist party has monopolized power and determined policy in the Soviet Union for thirty-five years. Stalin built it into that monolithic strength, and has left it strong. The proclamation of his death to the peoples of Russia and the several summons to unity unctuously put the party forward as the sole pillar of national support in what otherwise would be a national crisis. The party remains intact. It met no breath of challenge to the assumptions of its spokesmen. It should be noted too that the fundamentals of party purpose and policy had review and reaffirmation in the Party Congress no longer ago than October, 1952. That the funeral orations of the new leaders were a further definition of fundamental party doctrine.

The readiness and precision with which party and government adjustments were announced afford evidence enough that they reflected decisions taken earlier with Stalin alive and approving. With two exceptions at most, even the personnel roster consists of men he had hand picked, brought to posts of power and trained in party policy.

What Communists call by the euphemism "democratic centralization," under Stalin's leadership had for long lodged all operative power of the government in the party and in the party in the same handful of men styled the Political Bureau. This last the October Congress renamed Presidium and more than doubled in full members and alternates. In the current shuffle the new name held up, but the membership was cut down to the more manageable old dimension. The gears of State likewise were tightened. Ministries were combined. Trustworthy Old Guarders received dual offices. And the Supreme Soviet swallowed the whole prescription unanimously without a murmur of dissent after forty-seven minutes of oratory intended for public consumption.

Three seasoned figures appear fashioned into a sort of joint keystone of the arch of authority—often dubbed the triumvirate. Two of them have well established records. Our own Secretary of State rates the new Foreign Minister Molotov's diplomatic performance in the London Conference of Foreign Ministers as the most skilled in his experience. The tough Beria emerged from the furious purge of the 1930's as top executioner of the doomed and the keeper of internal order. Soviet international and domestic affairs will enjoy regularity and security in their orthodox hands. As for Malenkov, the wildest stretch of one's imagination would not permit of the presumption that Stalin would elevate to the top post a man disposed to wander in any degree from the time-honored and successful courses of his patron and teacher. The alignment in its entirety speaks for continuity of basic established policies.

But no ready-made dictator steps into the empty shoes. The West has now to deal with a team of individuals probably lesser in stature and surely less secure in their individual roles than the former dominating figure. If a great one be among them in the making, time will be required for him to gain real mastery. It took Stalin many years to reach his singleness of power. And at what prices both within Russia and in the world of nations.

The situation rationally prescribes to the Kremlin leadership for the immediate future familiar paths pursued by familiar ways. The recently announced economic development accord between Red China and the Kremlin illustrates very well what can be expected. That union of forces and resources under the propulsion of well established Stalin policies proves this point.

Yet, with the trusted chief gone, caution rather than innovation can be expected as the normal manifestation of unaccustomed responsibility. If one anticipated a great new idea or phrase in Kremlin utterances since the master-voice went silent, he has looked for it in vain. This holds true whether it be the glorying in communism and the party achievements, on coexistence with capitalism, identification with the revolutionaries at war with western states, or open doors to negotiation and loudly professed dedication to peace. Small comfort will be drawn from Malenkov's pledge to the Supreme Soviet in respect to "observance of established international norms." That was the very week chosen for free-hand shooting at American and British planes.

With the omens adding up so uniformly to a basic "as you were," there is propriety and need in a steady look at the Russia we face now, and will continue to face as the days ensue. Such a look will serve to highlight related events, to account for them, and to lead on to rational anticipations. What will be found significant is a body of data and of realistic interpretation essential as a guide to comprehension of what takes place. In the study that follows is lodged the kernel of what could prove to be rewarding approaches to an eventual peaceful show-down between East and West.

"The Russia We Face Now" comes packed with authentic information and reasonable deductions reached from first-hand experience, from access to original documents, and from consultation with competent specialists in government and with others versed in public affairs. It carries reliable objective evidence sufficient to support the positions taken. Backstopping both is a wealth of material omitted in order to keep the main lines clearly before the reader unencumbered with a mass of detail.

The central position is that the Soviet government is committed to the Marx-Lenin-Stalin doctrine of world communism to be achieved through a world revolution that must destroy democracy and any other opposing form of political organization; that the Soviet government has not changed its purposes in this direction since the Bolshevist seizure of power in 1917; that understanding this now is the first essential step in developing an adequate policy and program for meeting this Russia.

There follows an examination of why Russia holds so tenaciously to this singleness of purpose. Out of this excursion emerge certain observations that may prove helpful in reaching a lasting world peace.

This book is unique among analyses of contemporary Russia. It is made so by the method used in producing it. The account is a composite of the knowledge and thinking of a substantial group of persons equipped to reach and to express well considered judgments on Soviet Russian policies and practices. They represent unusual first-hand acquaintanceship with Soviet Russia dating from 1917. They have followed its development and operations unremittingly inside and outside. Their collaboration has been complete. While one author has been responsible for the book in its entirety, every word has been subjected to the critical scrutiny of the others. As each of the associates brought to the task insights from different backgrounds of experience, the production has been enriched materially in the process.

Authorship has rested primarily with Dr. Ethan T. Colton. It would be hard, indeed, to find any American possessing a more ripe and systematic knowledge of Russia, or who has maintained a more consistent calm and balance throughout the tense years of changing Soviet relationships. When the Bolsheviks undertook to propagandize the outside world with a wide spread of the Preobranzhansky-Bukharin book, "The A B C of Communism," it was Dr. Colton's "The X Y Z of Communism," published by Macmillan in 1931, that established what takes place when men who believe the ABC's get power and go to work on the pattern. The London Times credited him with applying "the impartiality of the practical man."

Dr. Colton was responsible for the direction, on Russian ground and from the home base, of two widespread American service organizations extending from 1918 through the next decade. In these managerial capacities he acquired workaday familiarity with Soviet and party gearings that escape the tourist spectator or the academic inquirer.

Dr. Dewey Anderson, Executive Director of the Public Affairs Institute of Washington, D. C. conceived and designed the collaboration. He was one of the last two famine relief officers to work in Russia. He later took a Ph.D. minor in Slavic Studies at Stanford University, where the Hoover War Library contains the world's greatest accessible wealth of first-hand materials. He has actively maintained the scholar's interest in Russian developments since then. Responsible positions in Washington during the past fourteen years have given him wide opportunities to observe and get the feel of unfolding international relations between our country and the Soviet government, checked against intercepts and official documents.

The group set themselves the task of determining what any body of competent men, who approached the facts of Soviet Russia's foreign policies in an objective manner, would conclude concerning the Kremlin's real intentions past and present. Once having established this, they have gone on to explore practical measures the free world could take to preserve democracy, and to secure ascendency over the totalitarian ideological dictatorship that stretches out from the Kremlin. Their realism rules out easy or quick results. They see us involved in prolonged and costly struggle. They objectify unshaken faith in democracy and dedication to the worldwide ends of freedom and peace.

A SHOCK INTO REALISM

What Ten Costly Years Taught Us

Failure to know the true nature of the Russia we face has made the past ten years among the most costly in our whole national life.

Failure to appraise adequately and in time the Kremlin connections with the Chinese Communists, and the relations of both to the world revolutionary purposes of Moscow. These played no small part in the victorious emergence of China's merciless dictatorship and Mao's steadfastness in the passing of Stalin.

Failure to understand the meaning of Russian sovietizing of North Korea caused our premature withdrawal of military defense forces and the open invitation to military aggression that followed in South Korea.

General Matthew Ridgway, straight from his contact with the Korean front of world communism, summed up its meaning to the Congress of the United States as "a warning as menacing and as urgent as a forest fire bearing down on a wooden village."

Here stand out boldly recent costly mistakes in the East.

In Europe it took such overt events as the guerilla warfare in Greece to awaken this government and people to realization of the undeviating purposes and program of the Kremlin. Both labored under the assumption that dealings with the Soviet government would be on terms of more or less normal diplomacy—by mutual concessions. How else explain the hazardous, and, as it turned out, nearly fatal experiment in four power cooperation? For no well balanced American believes there was intention to favor Soviet interests per se at the price of sacrificing our own.

The early ruptures of Yalta and Potsdam agreements were signals of more to come. In the long roster of failures to command observance of pledges by Moscow, the following are important to recall:

Failure to remain well armed in the immediate postwar confusion period, resulting in an irresistible invitation to the Kremlin to strengthen its own borders by the forceful establishment of a ring of satellite nations integrated into the Communist system.

Failure to anticipate the interactions between war-shaken economic stability and free political institutions. So that the desperate postwar conditions which developed in most countries of Europe were an opportunity not overlooked for a day by the agents and affiliates of Moscow-directed world communism.

Failure to save free Czechoslovakia. The chance may have been ours for one brief moment following the war. Had we and our government known Soviet policies and purposes sufficiently well, "the boys would not have been brought home" overnight. Military strength on the ground or near at hand and ready to back up the Benes' government, if threatened by outside armed force, could have given that democratic government the power it needed to prevent the rise of communism from within and withstand successfully the ruthless pressure exerted from Moscow. Czechoslovakia would have been a Marshall Plan participant and otherwise have materially changed the whole course of postwar history in Europe.

Failure to understand and appraise correctly the meaning of Stalin's death and the transfer of power to his successors. This caused confusion amongst us, vain hope of internal disorders and disintegration of the Soviet Empire, costly indecision in the formulation of foreign policy vis-a-vis the Kremlin.

We need not have made these many failures which have cost so much in human lives, suffering, wealth and anxiety. We need not commit now the failure of losing Iran for the free world, which could add another $10 billions a year to our defense bill alone. We need not make other failures that are presently a-building—in India, Africa and elsewhere, which play into the Kremlin hands. But we will surely make these failures as we have those of the past unless we accurately appraise the purposes and plans of the Russia we face.

The fundamental fact emerges that we in America cannot expect to develop an effective policy or program of action vis-a-vis any Soviet government, old or new, without knowing beyond peradventure what all along has motivated Kremlin leadership, and will inspire no less Stalin's survivors in the party Presidium. Accordingly, no Washington Administration, no State Department chief, no career service experts, nor their advisors should be expected to move farther out into the "no man's land" of vital Soviet relations than a public made fully aware of the hazards will be found prepared to cope with when the realities show up.

The documentation required to build the robust realism that might have averted these failures has reposed abundantly in the archives of every non-Russian chancellery. As it lay dormant in the files of the governments across the free world, what Arthur Krock calls the "calamitous mistake" was made in predicting the course the men in the Kremlin would take in international relations.

To fix responsibility for what has occurred on a political party or individual basis misfires. For if leadership in either of our great parties, in or out of office, enjoyed superior wisdom when the great civil and military decisions were debated and taken, except in a few isolated instances, it was conspicuous by its silence. It is not in the realm of assessing guilt that profit is to be taken by those of us who are concerned to establish right policies now. It is in

2

interpreting correctly the meaning for the future of the Kremlin's past and current actions that the hope lies.

All of us suffer from a great reluctance to face the grim facts of the present world situation. A bipartisan majority in the House of Representatives went from listening to General Ridgway's first-hand report on the meaning of Korea to vote a savage, if not vindictive, cut in major defense expenditures. In Europe an understandable but excessive "neutralism" is supported sufficiently to weaken national defense policies. As though no organized militant force operates across the world with the deliberate purpose of destroying the civilized order of free government and free society. As though this force were not making startling advances in the face of our bewilderment.

The Iron Will and Unshakeable Program

Central among stern lessons is the bitter finding that, however much or little the Stalin's, Malenkov's, Molotov's, Vishinsky's (and genuine comrades anywhere) will yield at times to terms bargained with non-Communist forces, the results cannot be regarded as final settlements. For they never forsake the iron will and ultimate program for throwing down the entire political, economic and social world order against which they have sworn destruction until, as Lenin put it, "not one stone is left on another." That includes, let it be understood this time, the physical extinction of opposition, wholesale and individual. Their faithless agreements stand up only until the opportunity arises to resume assaults at the identical places where they were stopped in their line.

The postwar aftermath in Eastern Europe affords an illuminating chapter. In what Mr. Byrnes calls a "genial atmosphere" the big three chiefs of state at Yalta in February, 1945, pledged themselves "to concert, during the temporary period of instability in liberated Europe, the policies of their three governments in assisting the peoples liberated from the domination of Nazi Germany and the peoples of the former Axis satellite states of Europe to solve *by democratic means* their pressing political and economic problems."

Stalin waited eight days from the signing before he dispatched Vishinsky to Bucharest to commit political mayhem on the representative legal Rumanian government. His agents manhandled Polish affairs with parallel effrontery, equal thoroughness and more brutality. Down the corridor from the Baltic to the Black and Aegean seas no independent political party or institution has survived, not even the Communist party if the first adjective be respected.

The economies of 100,000,000 people have been revolutionized and geared into the Soviet Union system for control and systematic exploitation. The former accepted leadership has been destroyed by imprisonment and execution or flight from terror into exile. Dictatorship over learning and thinking

3

imposes itself on the national cultures of the ages, intent on their destruction. A program of militarization under Soviet inspiration and command dates from the signing of peace treaties that prescribed strict limitations. The voluminous reminders to the Kremlin of its commitments by London and Washington might as well have been addressed to the four winds of space. Moscow had the power at hand and all three governments knew it. The international highwaymen proceeded unilaterally according to plan, as their history establishes they will wherever and whenever opportunity offers across the world.

Nor is there any evidence that this iron will and unshakeable program has undergone fundamental change with the passing of Stalin. As will be discussed later, the Kremlin's purpose is not to be assumed from any momentary technique or strategy they may employ. Thus, it suits them on occasion to assume the most friendly of manner, to advocate the most engaging of peaceful policies, to seek world friendship. In the very next moment, as historic time is judged, they may launch a virulent campaign of vituperation and hatred. The target of these diametrically opposed tactics may be entirely fooled unless he is thoroughly grounded in the fundamentals of Communist purposes and completely sophisticated about them.

Dedication to World Mission

The sense of mission to establish communism across the world inspires the ruling personalities and the faithful rank and file from the Iron Curtain to Tibet. Completely indoctrinated, they have been reared to this dedication. They employ endlessly the fighting air of their "Internationale" to summon the masses of every land to the class war. It appears to strike up spontaneously as if to signify the spirit of struggle on the march in all manner of assemblies from the Supreme Soviet to funerals. The opening lines run:

> "Arise ye prisoners of starvation!
> Arise ye wretched ones of earth!
> For justice thunders condemnation—
> A better world's in birth."

The "A B C of Communism" (four English editions 1922 to 1927), widely translated and used for bottle feeding inquirers in elements of the faith and tactics, heralded a worldwide economic system and the time coming for the "creation of one world-wide Socialist republic."

In the 1923 Constitution, the Soviet fathers declared the Union to be "a decisive step toward the union of the toilers of all countries into one World Soviet Socialist Republic." That charter provided for the admission to the union of all existing Soviet Socialist Republics and "such as shall arise in the future."

4

The amended fundamental law of 1947 omits mention of an open door for new applications to union membership. Still the facility with which Lithuania, Latvia, Estonia, Bessarabia and the annexations from east Poland "gained admittance" (by propulsion) indicates a gate that easily swings ajar. Indeed the English text of this new Constitution, printed by the Foreign Languages Publishing House, Moscow, 1947, bearing the Hammer and Sickle official insignia, carries on the flyleaf the universally familiar call, "Workers of all countries, unite." The arms of the U.S.S.R. bear the same inscription. More than passing interest attaches to the omission of "Russia" from the name of the state that emerged from the October, 1917, revolution, thus avoiding geographical designation of its domain. No parallel to this device comes to mind. It squares with the proclamation of world mission as supreme purpose and duty.

The break of Stalin with Trotsky, Rykov, and the other comrade Bolsheviks of Lenin in the late 1920's and early '30's received wide publicity as Soviet abandonment of revolution on the world scale. That inference, if sought, never had substance. It pleased the gullible. What Stalin did was to take the masterful course of emphasis on the buildup of Soviet success and strength to such proportions as would instill confidence in the home population; impress the outer world; and be adequate for defense and, as it proved, for offense. The Third International carried on a quarter century in furtherance of Communist penetration and organization across the world with Russian party leaders dominant in the executive organ. Its promoters and their publicity blazoned the "Great" Stalin as "our matchless leader." They were never silenced nor even rebuked.

That particular instrument of revolution, shortened in common appellation to Comintern, went into the discard midway in World War II. By then it had served well its purposes in the original form and the dissolution made an excellent widely heralded contribution to Soviet high politics. The dissolving order stipulated that the act connoted in no wise repudiation of world revolution, yet it probably influenced important men on the higher levels of allied leadership into believing Soviet post-war cooperation would be forthcoming.

Day by day events meanwhile evidenced clearly that the dissolution had not released the formerly appending national parties from bonds to Moscow, and their manipulation by the Kremlin. Tito's assertion of independent administration in Jugoslavia brought down on him resounding charges of "traitor," noisy sword rattling over his border, and the giant Soviet-satellite economic squeeze of the militantly aggressive Cominform, new version of the Comintern which emerged in 1947. The appearance of the Cominform, only four years after the original machine had been scrapped, should have taught its lesson to those who heralded the liquidation of the old Comintern as a sign of fundamental changes in Soviet policy.

5

Stalin put Soviet Russia in a world setting and himself on record in his 1926 book, "On the Problems of Leninism." He quotes this passage from Lenin's statement to the Eighth Party Congress: "We are living not merely in a state but in a system of states, and the existence of the Soviet Republic side by side with imperialist states for a long time is unthinkable. One or the other must triumph in the end. And before that end supervenes, a series of frightful collisions between the Soviet Republic and the bourgeois states will be inevitable." Stalin then observes "Clear, one would think." The work has gone through eleven editions. The last appeared in 1945. It is today's doctrine!

Stalin further wrapped up his personal commitment on the subject of revolutionary aggression in a euphemism. The Party Congress of 1939 required an explanation for the large scale continuance of armed strength, penal agencies and the secret intelligence after "Socialism in one State" had been demonstrated (officially proclaimed in fact), the dispossessed classes at home suppressed, and the land successfully defended against foreign interventions. The need remained and would persist, he explained, until "the capitalist environment would be liquidated." Of the measures still irking the people, he said, "the point of their weapon is no longer directed inside the country, but outside it and against our enemies." The "pointed weapon" on missions of security has proved effective since 1945 up to the Elbe in central Germany in mid-Europe; to the Adriatic in the South; over 400,000,000 Chinese and Tibetans; and into the Himalayas on the India frontiers. It halts perforce only before the stand of the still free nations—the "unliquidated capitalist environment."

Malenkov boldly took up the torch of his teacher-trainer in the March 9th eulogy. He spoke a sentence on the Lenin-Stalin promise of possible "prolonged coexistence" of the Capitalist and Socialist systems in contrast to three paragraphs on the "mighty camp of peace, democracy and socialism" set up under the leadership of the fallen chief. The citation of unit members of the "camp" reveals its nature, objectives and strategies. For in it "march the great Chinese people, the fraternal peoples of Poland, Czechoslovakia, Bulgaria, Hungary, Rumania, Albania, the (East) German Democratic Republic and the Mongolian People's Republic." And for full measure the "heroic" Koreans and "courageous" Viet Namese. The "sacred task" confronted "to preserve and consolidate the greatest attainment of the people —the camp of peace, democracy and socialism . . ." And from the peroration:

"Toilers of the Soviet Union, see and know that our powerful fatherland is advancing toward new successes" . . .

"Forward, along the road toward the complete victory of the great cause of Lenin and Stalin."

The United States, Enemy No. 1

This Soviet system that we face thrusts its strength most specifically

6

against the United States as the counter-power standing across its path of expansion over the world, whether peacefully or otherwise. The logic and impulse of communist orthodoxy bring us to this inevitable historic position. The Russian people and government gained a world of good will by a gallant performance in the last war. Lively hope had been widely kindled that the building of One World, and a better one, would be sought in mutual confidence. A considerable measure of faith arose that more than sheer politics lay back of the Comintern's liquidation, the new Soviet constitution with its presumed "democratic" content, liberalizations toward the Russian Church, and certain assurances about coexistence released in the amiable interviews of the Generalissimo. Instead, from the Kremlin quarter, a creeping chill set in as soon as the course of the war insured victory over Germany.

Publicity and actions began to establish that the common danger had merely caused Moscow to suspend in wartime relations with the Allies the "enemy" concept that party indoctrination attaches to non-Communist states. The West kept getting sharp reminders that even in the crises the Kremlin's conduct showed distrust. Throughout the war, the exchange of technological military information had been mostly one-way traffic in Soviet direction. That authority took without giving. It kept allied military attachés, with few exceptions, well back from the fronts. Secrecy measures required the donated billions worth of aid material to be dumped at the borders and go forward solely by Soviet transport. The American Red Cross and Russian War Relief had no operative contact over the frontier despite their very large benefactions. Civilian air passengers, Russia bound, uniformly transferred at outside airports, there to take Soviet planes to their destination. Mountainous pressure on Moscow had failed to secure an inside base for landing and refueling Allied bombers on transcontinental missions until the concession (shortly revoked) came to have value for advancing Russian armies themselves. During its observance, our fliers while at Soviet terminals experienced virtual internment. The long denial cost us many fallen planes and fliers and spared the enemy much strafing.

Attitudes began taking on openly the old familiar expressions of suspicion, fear and hostility. Frederick C. Barghoorn, in "Annals of the American Academy of Political and Social Science" (May of 1949), gives a running account of the transition observed from his post of Attaché in our Moscow Embassy from 1942-47. Soviet officialdom and press, first quietly, then with rising accent, began depreciation of the Allies, their lesser shares in the martial achievements, their class economy, the false seductive bourgeois culture, the reactionaries among them influencing Western foreign policy against Soviet interests.

With these innuendos and charges mingled demands for the moral and political defeat of fascism across the world map. The build-up of defamation soon identified as fascists whoever did not go along the Soviet domestic and foreign line. By degrees the propaganda transferred the wicked seat and bulwark of fascism from Nazi Germany to "imperialistic" America. The formula advanced to the endangered socialist land in a hostile capitalist world. Kalinin, then alive and in the Presidential office, warned in a widely circulated speech against any illusion that "all danger to our State structure and social order" disappeared "in the victory."

The claims for bases in the name of "security" reached out for posts on the Bosporus, in the Aegean sea and on the central North African coast. By that time bargaining temperatures were cooling in the conference halls. The once obliging Allies said "no." The Council of Foreign Ministers in London deadlocked over Molotov's defiant demands. Since then declared "cold war" replaced what had passed for collaboration. The United States gets caricatured to mankind as Warmongering Enemy Number One. Stalin, in time of need, told Harry Hopkins that President Roosevelt and the United States had more influence with the common people of the world than any other force. What could be more important and necessary now than to have our international prestige countered with abuse, insults and lies, and our national strength isolated and hamstrung?

Or, if Soviet strategy dictates a change of pace and apparent direction, that the United States just as suddenly becomes something other than Enemy Number One? Only this is unlikely so long as the basic elements of Communist drives dominate Kremlin leadership and policies. We are fated to be Number One on Malenkov's enemy list for a long time to come strictly because as the strongest democracy we offer the greatest threat to the accomplishment of the Kremlin's purpose. This stems from the undeviating party line doctrine hallowed by Lenin.

RUSSIA'S POWER AND HER DRIVES

The Land Base

Primary among the power assets to be reckoned with in this hostile quarter are those deriving from the land and its resources. These provide wherewithal for almost limitless might. The territory of majestic dimensions spans 6,000 miles of latitude across half of Europe and all of Asia. An inland sea has one and a half times the surface of the five Great Lakes of our home continent. Four of the world's nine largest rivers that course over 2,800 miles run entirely in this domain.

No one of the continents is underlain with an equal range and quantity of known mineral deposits. Ranking by nations puts the Russo-Siberian findings first in iron (with quartzites). Similarly in manganese, phosphorites, magnesium, apatite and peat. The standing in coal, lead, nickel and zinc is second. Large hydraulic assets augment the foregoing power potentials. A third of the global timber stands in the Russian forests. Some limiting factors intrude. While the square mileage just about equals that of all North America, the arable portions total less, and vast Arctic spaces are unhabitable. Natural limitation to food production looms in no far future.

The People

The human dwellers over this rich patrimony number nearly 200,000,000. Their new born millions yearly give them a rating among the world's most prolific peoples. The mass breaks down into something like 200 ethnic units. Each has its own language or dialect in which the primary school books are printed. Many of them may be dismissed as negligible in respect to more than tribal influence. The major groups call for particulars either in population, material assets, or strategic position, or these in combination.

Slavs account for slightly more than three-fourths of the total. Of these two-thirds come under the "Great Russian" category. They form the large majority in the European Russian heartland, then reach out the controlling arm across Central Asia and Siberia. Since the buildup from the ruin worked by the Tartars in the XIIIth century, this element has dominated public affairs. It so continues through preponderant weight in the Communist party.

The 35,000,000 Ukranians (Little Russians) living in the Southwest European quarter rate next in importance in their own right. Russian culture first germinated and flourished there. Likewise the Russian State,

9

until Kiev as capital on the historic Dneiper river yielded the ruling primacy to interior Moscow. A strong Ukranian spirit of independence survived. Fed on discontent with a secondary role in all-Russian affairs, tangential tendencies away from Moscow centralization persistently manifest themselves. The initial defection of Ukranians to the German invaders in 1941 were of significant proportions. Agriculture and industry in the Ukraine present the best economic balance in the Soviet Union. The Kremlin Government could ill afford its actual alienation.

A buffer area shouldering against Poland, called Byelorussia (White) historically, had a major Polish population (before deportations) along with large Ukranian elements and lesser Lithuanian and Jewish minorities. A chief value to the Soviet Union lies in the geographical position. Wars to possess this area between Poles, Swedes, Tartars, Germans, Lithuanians and all the Russian strains have blood-soaked the soil.

Stalin wrote off the centuries long claim of Poland, but others will rise up to speak for the Poles as did Matushevski of the now silenced Gazeta Polska: "They are Polish lands. Many more Poles were killed by Tartar arrows, Turkish scimitars, Austrian bullets or Russian bayonets in the defense of Lvov than live in that city today. Ours are the Polesian plains and marshes. The forests and cemeteries of those lands, their very breeze and contour, are Polish. There is only one way of compelling the Polish nation to surrender its freedom or its land—and that is to exterminate the Poles to the last man."

The far westward thrust of Peter the Great (1701-1721) incorporated the three small Baltic lands of non-Slavs into his Empire. Estonia, Latvia and Lithuania have been retained under Russian rule except for the period between the two World Wars and a brief time of occupation by German armies. Their possession posts any Moscow government securely on the Baltic Sea.

On the Transcaucasian Southern border three non-Slavic small peoples make up the base population—by name, Georgians, Armenians and Azerbaidzhanians. These ancient stocks, rooted in history, proud of race, have been accorded each its own national status in the state structure up on the level of Union Republics as contrasted with subsidiary autonomous republics, autonomous regions, and national areas. Their lands afford strategic spaces for defense and advance positions for offense vis-a-vis Iran, Turkey and the Middle East. The population includes withal sizeable Persian and Turkish elements.

The lands of Mongoloid peoples, displayed in distinctive colors across Central Asia and Siberia on the broad pattern of Slavic population, give a map of Soviet Russia the semblance of a crazy-quilt. The patches dominate the racial scene from the Volga valley to the Japan, Okhotsk and Bering seas, and from the mid-Asian mountain barrier to the 3,500 miles of Arctic shore line. Five of them in particular occupy pivotal mid-Asian positions. These major groups range in area from 55,000 to 1,560,000 square miles, in population from 1,254,000 to 6,300,000.

The Turkmen (former Russian Turkistan) southern frontier coincides with half the Iranian north line. Uzbek bounds Afganistan on its north side except where Tadjik takes up. Tadjik then goes on to counter an arc of the Indian border. Tadjik, Kirghiz and Kazakh all abut on Sinkiang, the vulnerable far northwestern province of China. Across their frontiers the long Soviet arm has attained dominant influence. The border penetrations date back to Tsarist days. Soviet policy has steadily advanced them. China's life and death struggle with the forces of Japan furthered Moscow's objective in giving a free hand to establish virtual authority over the economy and government of that great Chinese possession. The fate of vast Outer Mongolia awaits it, where, without full status in the Soviet Union, a total suzerainty has been established. Only a breach with Mao at Peiping might avert it for Sinkiang, and it is late for that.

Preoccupation of the West with Europe and the Far East serves to deflect attention from the enterprises of the Soviet government at this very strategic center of Asia, generally dismissed as remote, arid, nomadic in economy and benighted. Nehru knows better. The British also. They did something about it in their strength, stood guard at the Kyber Pass and before Tibet, and resisted pressures on the Afghans. The men in the Kremlin are engaged in large scale proprietary action. They have development plans for projects in each of the five Republics that make the United States Technical Assistance program for Asia feeble by comparison.

Irrigation, mechanized agriculture, the disciplines of collective farming and industrial installations are transforming the old nomadic life into a modern economy. Large scale production is being built up in cotton, rubber, silk, hemp and tobacco, all formerly dependent on imports or done without. Parallel increases have come in cereals, fruits and beet sugar. Stock farms for sheep, goats and cattle breeding step up meat, dairy, hide and wool supplies. Textile mills, canneries and packing plants on the ground process the raw materials. Vigorous prospecting has located oil and a wealth of other minerals. Drilling, mining and smelters followed. New railways thrust into the interiors and up to the frontiers. One of them crosses over into extreme northwest China.

The program has varied objectives, among them increases of area and all-Union commodities, independence from imports and security whether offensive or defensive. Withal the Communist party entrenches its power in an industrial worker class. Where such does not exist industries must be created, whether or not they are economic naturals. For this and other ends huge capital funds of the Five Year Plans have been plowed into these formerly pastoral and primitively agrarian regions. Industrialization is on the

11

march across Siberia from the Urals to the maritime provinces marked by such giants as the Magnitogorsk, Kuznetz, Lena and Tetukhe developments. Strategically these have located immense military potentials farther from anybody's bombers.

Pre-Soviet Expansion

The fanning out of Slavs from the Dneiper valley strip over a dominion that reaches from mid-Europe to the Pacific ocean, and into it, took well over a millenium. The tempo of expansion was never that of uninterrupted marches forward. Advance and recession alternated. World War II produced conditions for a major bulge. No previous decade saw Russian territorial gains of consequence marked up equal to those of 1940-50. And the Kremlin high pressures the neighbors on all the cardinal points except the north. There only the Arctic Ocean remains to be occupied. If this expansion is not a carry-over from the old imperialism in part, the effects on world order and peace are parallel.

The Russian nation, as already noted, had its genesis along the middle Dnieper, chief artery of the great ancient trade route traceable on a current map from the Gulf of Finland into Lake Ladoga by the Neva, along the Volkhov river south to Novgorod (on Lake Ilmen), up another water course to a portage over into the Dnieper, on to the Black Sea and Constantinople. Kiev in the South became the city of distinction economically and politically. Though for centuries cut off from Western Europe by the intervening Lithuanian and Polish empires, its status in power, wealth and culture in the 11th century was comparable with most of the capitals of western Europe.

The tornadic storm (out of Asia) of Genghis Khan's warriors brought state and civilization down in disaster. Kiev fell in 1240, and along with all other cities in the path was looted and burned after the Tartar pattern. The impact, together with quarreling claimants to the rule, split the surviving population three ways. The land divisions have carried down as the Little, White and Great Russias. The respective peoples addressed themselves to life anew either in the ruins, or migrated into the wilderness.

Moscow in the deep forest area drew settlers from a wide periphery and came to sufficient power to lead in throwing back the Tartars after 240 years of their overlordship and tribute. From what became the Duchy of Moscow evolved the domain of Great Russians and the Tsarist imperium. Slav settlement slowly advanced across Siberia after 1600, paced by adventurers, traders, persecuted Old Believers, Cossacks given land for services to the Tsars, and political exiles. Military strength was exerted at times. Not much was required up to the Manchurian enterprise at the turn into the XXth century—less than our forefathers employed to disposses the Mexicans and Indians and incorporate their lands into the American union. Catherine II activated a parallel case of "Manifest Destiny," by pushing the Turks from the north and east Black Sea coasts, except that the Turks, there as earlier conquerors, fought back. Absorption of the Transcaucasians waited until the mid-XIXth century.

In contrast the tide of power on the western borders ebbed and flowed ceaselessly. The neighboring Poles and Lithuanians pressed in for rule and settlement, the Swedes for conquest and trade. For 736 years from A.D. 869 the Russians had a ruling line of non-Slav origin, the Ruriks of Norsemen stock (early Slavicized to be sure). They came to the role of power by invitation of the people in a time of disordered economy and leadership. In 1605 the line failed to provide a member for the succession. The "Time of Trouble" ensued, compounded by the ambitious Boris Gudonoff, the "false Dmitri" hoax, and the last thrust of the Polish King at Russia, this time to seize the throne itself. As in former crises, Russian character made the rebound to order and momentum after a despairing decade. An assembly summoned for the choice of an acceptable Tsar elected Michael Romanov.

The Romanov dynasty dating from 1613 first brought about stabilization, and from there launched aggressions against the weakening neighbors. It relentlessly pressured the Poland of the time to its doom, first out of all lands east of the Dnieper, then from the long contested buffer zones, finally with Prussia and Austria executing the ruthless triple partitionings (1772, 1792-1795). Peter the Great had set Charles XII of Sweden back on his heels in 1709 when that King's ambition propelled him deep into the Ukraine at the ultimate cost of his Finnish and Baltic holdings. Crecy listed Poltava, scene of the crucial Swedish defeat in the Ukraine, in his "Fifteen Decisive Battles of the World." Thus latterly in the XVIIIth century the Russian Slav had arrived at security in his own house, had successfully taken on continental offensives, had appeared in Berlin in 1760, and stood poised for further exploits.

A "Class A" Power

From here forward Russian governments sat in on the major power games vis-a-vis their European opposites and Turkey. They dealt both in and out of coalitions. Their armies measured up with the best of Prussia and France. No generals outclassed Suvarov or Kutuzov, fighting vs France's revolutionary armies and Napoleon. Stalin's Russians are not the first to occupy the capitals of beaten European states. Alexander I kept 27,000 of his troops for several years in Paris after helping to undo Napoleon, Italy and Prussia.

Intermittently, the pressure of this Slav power gravely troubled western chancelleries, notably when exerted in the southeast to accelerate Turkish exodus from the Balkans and fill in the power vacuum. "Liberation" of the Balkan Slavs from the Sultans was more than a cliche. Russia did more to bring that about than all the rival powers opposing her. The imperial objectives, however, included Russian hegemony over the Balkan peoples and footing athwart the Dardanelles where the British, French and Austrians had important stakes. The British and French provoked the Crimean War and upset the Russian timetable. In the 1878 settlement of the Russo-Turkish War, the three powers pooled diplomacy to despoil the Tsar of the fruits of victory. Bismarck for Prussia took the role of "honest" broker to avert a continental war.

The British took yet longer views as Russian expansion policies reached out beyond the Straits, toward Persia, Central Asia and along the northern Chinese perimeter of Sinkiang, Mongolia and Manchuria. At every thrust of the Great Slav toward warm seaways, Britain countered with her own diplomatic weight backed by the world's chief navy in reserve. Japan joined in resistance on the Pacific side to win a temporarily deterring war in Manchuria in 1904. To this the United States had lent moral and civilian financial support. The first President Roosevelt engineered the Portsmouth peace without any thanks in the end from either combatant.

Soviet Expansion Dynamic

Regardless of the extent to which Soviet foreign policy in these 1950's shall be considered as imperialistic nationalism in character, the geographic pattern of achievement thus far matches pretty much that of the Romanovs, area by area, only more amply. The penetration of this new power has advanced farther than the Tsars' along the Baltic into Germany proper; across all East Europe and deeply into the mid-Continent; over most of the Balkans; back into Manchuria; by proxy in Tibet and all China; and into the Kurile Pacific islands on Japan's flank—advance stepping stones up toward Alaska. On alert for good measure, the Kremlin eyes and ears look out and listen over Iran, the Arab states including those of North Africa. Western negotiators received an awakening jolt in the first top level conference room where the Soviet member spoke up for a place in Lybia's sun. John Foster Dulles has observed that "never before have so few gained so much so fast."

The old offsets to Russian power being no longer present in their former capacity highly magnifies the new acquisitions in importance. The one time German-Austrian barrier that long contained it on the west is down. In so far as Teutonic strength goes at this moment in history, the Soviet power may sally forth when and as far as it chooses. The Arab world is defenceless by itself. Britain stands no more on the Indian Northwest frontier. At sea she is not now mistress enforcing the Pax Britannica. The victors of 1946 disarmed the Japanese, pledged them constitutionally to pacifism. They now lead them into measures for defense of the Far East against threatened Communist aggressions. Just as paradoxically, after destruction of the German's military power, the West seeks its partial restoration as a buttress to security against further Soviet revolutionary advances in Europe.

The spread of imperial Russian power over one-sixth of the earth's land surface had the design in general of its contemporary imperialisms. Variables in the Romanov pattern from that of the Orleans, Hapsburg, Tudor and Hanover Houses were not in essential characteristics. The Tsarist Slavs pressured themselves over the half of both Europe and Asia, the Anglo-Saxons over the seven seas, the French deeply into Africa. All remained substantially in a common world order of society. Then this new, strange, world-minded, imperious Communist force exploded on the continental scene.

Revolutionary Russia proved prepared ground as a propagating base at the close of World War I. Here was something different among imperialisms—a new species materialized out of the teachings that Karl Marx authored in the mid-1800 decades. Organizationally, the Marxist ideas in the main had taken form in what came to be familiar as moderate Socialist parties, democratic in procedure for achievement of the aims, evolutionary in program. They had flamed up in the Paris Commune of 1871 into violence and bloodshed, fanned by a school of leaders who proclaimed seizure of power by direct mass action at the barricades.

Though smothered down in France and kept underground elsewhere, that conspiratorial revolutionary type in the great cities of Europe outlived suppression with the kindling potency of buried embers. Vladimir Ilich Ulyanov (1870-1924), a radical Russian student starting with doctrinaire Marxism and lessons from the Paris Commune's collapse, fashioned his own smashing Bolshevik program and, for its execution, a militant Communist party of Russians and Russian born comrades.

It may not be reckoned accidental that the man who did this and succeeded in doing what others failed of doing elsewhere, was a Russian. Certain conditions readied Russian society for being seized upon and made into the carrier of imported Western communism. They bred a Russian to see and grasp the opportunity. To use nurserymen's terms, the already Revolutionary Russia at the turn into the XXth century presented the "stock" on which Lenin and his handful of Bolsheviks grafted communism. The Century dictionary defines the grafting process and product as the insertion of a part of a plant in a slit of another plant "so as to become nourished by and united with it, the scion usually bearing flowers, fruit, etc., like the plant from which it was taken, and the stock usually retaining its own chacteristics."

The Russian Orthodox Church has implanted in the masses of faithful its own mystical Messianic sense—spiritual atmosphere congenial to the ideas of world mission. These impregnated political and cultural thought in a measure. Centuries of cruel invasions have schooled the people to ready defense of themselves against outside enemies. The Soviet regime makes a cardinal virtue and necessity of protection of the Socialist fatherland from the ring of hostile imperialists. The same masses gave immemorial acceptance of unitary, concentrated rule at the top. No earthquaking shock, indeed little or none, would attend transition of authority over their life from Tsarist autocracy to a Party Central Committee, Politburo and heroized Lenin or Stalin. The primacy and priority of the state over their well-being as individuals would be simply the projection of long experience, as would even a prying, ubiquitous political police system for securing the state's supremacy. Thus the Russian "stock" with sweat, sacrifice and suffering nourishes the successfully effected graft for a dynamic world embracing conspiracy, without (a minority excepted) being party to the plot.

In whatever degree resident Russian nationalism lends support to Soviet thrusts for expansion, these have a new and featured character. A revolutionary dynamic supercharges them. The movements suggest tiger-like ferocity and agility rather than the sheer lumbering weight of the once symbolic Bear. The objective of revolution generates jet propulsion into new territory. Major significance resides in the fact that progressively each achievement of Soviet political power over fresh territory accrues at the same time to its integrated revolutionary world order.

Communist revolutionary changes uniformly attend the imposition of Soviet authority whether within the U.S.S.R. or without, as in the European satellites. Former leadership that does not escape meets destruction. Institutions of the existing society that cannot be revamped to the ends of "proletarian culture" become relegated to limbo when not uprooted. Learning, thinking and their expression fall under dictatorship. Much legislation prescribes the possessions permitted each individual, harnesses his productive energy, controls the fruits of his labor, and by legalized wages and prices subordinates his housing, food and clothing to the will of the state in the persons of a Communist Party Political Bureau taking orders from Moscow. This is current history written into day by day events in Poland, Czechoslovakia, Hungary, Rumania and the rest of satellite Europe. A like program proceeds in China true to type.

Where Soviet Power Resides

The authors and directors of this and of all Soviet policy have their footing in the all-Union Communist Party of the Bolshevist color. No power, in principle or by statute in or outside the State apparatus, exists other than in that one existing party of some 6,882,000 members. Further a Political Bureau (Politburo) of the party, ranging numerically around a dozen men including alternates came into sole control by the managing skill of Joseph Stalin. The Party Congress of 1952 renamed this organ Presidium, but it is the same "rose." Under Lenin's premiership, control lay in the hands of a State organ—the Council of People's Commissars. With the Politburo at the apex of real power, the administration and political dualism between Soviet government and party threatened potentially the fabric of the Communist regime and was replaced, de facto, by the existing monolithic system now to be described.

The shift became visible soon after Lenin died, although no changes were made formally in the texts of the government and party constitutions. Those twelve or thirteen men of the Politburo emerged as an impersonal group with Stalin as its master. In common parlance, "Politburo" and "Stalin" came to have the same connotation for Russians as well as for the rest of the world. Obviously, if there had been left an element of democracy anywhere in the system, it would be found only in the Politburo itself. In fact, it is known that its decisions were made by voting. That probably mattered little if Stalin were there.

His position, however, varied in degree. When Stalin fought Trotsky's leftist opposition in the 1920's, he had to fall back on the support of Premier Rykov and the friends who sat with Rykov in the Politburo and made up the right wing of the party. In those years Stalin played the game according to rules, at least superficially, making certain concessions to the Rightists. In the 30's, though, he seems to have been throughout the Politburo's unchallenged master.

There are good reasons to assume that after 1945 the Politburo became the battlefield between two factions, Stalin leading the minority, against Zdanov who died in 1948 (a not always accepted natural death). It would be practically impossible to ascertain the exact degree to which Zdanov, making use of the Cominform, prevailed over Stalin in pushing further and further the annexationist policies in which the Soviet government was engaged at the time. It is certain that the Poliburo split, and what is more at this point, Stalin conformed with the letter of the "democratic" procedure, permitting himself to be out-voted. By showing such moderation, he might have wished to create a firm precedent, an established tradition, that may keep in bounds any fights for a like supremacy since his death.

The XIXth Congress of the party in October, 1952, changed the name of this supremely regnant organ to "Presidium," and increased its size to twenty-five full members and eleven alternates. No one on the outside, accredited with ripe knowledge of party and Soviet history, has spoken up otherwise than in certainty that the verbal changes signified no lessening of authority and control by the small established inner group. Instead, the Presidium took over the dissolved "Organization Bureau's" functions in the prime political area of party admissions, tenure, disciplines and advances. The new Party Control Committee, a fortnight after the Congress adjournment, dutifully elected to the Presidium all sitting Politburo members except one. The Stalin-Malenkov-Molotov-Beria line-up stayed intact. The recruits knew they owed their places to their tested loyalty to the Old Guard and its policies. Even so, their elevation proved transitory. The March 6th radio announcement of reorganization named a membership of ten for this Presidium body—eight of them the familiar Old Guard stalwarts. (Let the reader take note that in our further context throughout, the familiar Politburo name will be retained whenever it befits and identifies the related historical actions and events).

When Napoleon III was advanced from President of the French Republic to Emperor by a constitutional "change" in 1850, M. Kerr, a journalist in Paris, wrote "the more it changes the more it remains the same thing." The epigram, since repeated on innumerable occasions, applies admirably to these alterations in the framework of Soviet rule.

The Buro's self-execution in name could not possibly have meant that the extraordinary body was leaving the scene or changing its character. If this were the case, it would have meant revolution truly, rather than rearrangement in form and nomenclature. After the Politburo's period of control, Russia could not do suddenly without a closely knit power center such as ruled it for the past quarter of a century. The Politburo members simply screened themselves in the swollen company of the thirty-six members and alternates crowding the Presidium. The accessions probably were regarded in the way for post-Stalin eventualities. Such maneuvers are on the order of that political psychology in which the Kremlin has shown itself perspicacious before. Originally, the Secret Police had been named "Extraordinary Commission for the Combat of Spies, Speculators and Sabateurs," the initials being used to spell "Cheka" of dread repute. Three changes in appellation have taken place, without essential alteration functionally, and none in character. The succession will be identified here by the initials O.G.P.U., N.K.V.D., and the contemporary M.V.D. that now is imbedded in the Ministry of Interior under Beria.

In another case the people's one time Commissariats were made "Ministries," their Commissars "Ministers" at the war's end—a somewhat puzzling measure as it imitates bourgeois parlance. In this manner the Kremlin renders less conspicuous the official institutions, by unburdening them of the odious connotations which they contract at home—and the world over. Such normality will also stand it in good stead wherever it annexes a new country to the Communist imperium.

By the party constitutional definition, authority derives from its Congress. Prior to 1952, the body had met last in 1939; before that annually, or in alternate years. The Central Committee of the party, formerly numbering some seventy members, had once been the most powerful debating body both in the party and in the country, then came to be concerned mainly with party affairs. Pro forma, it chose the members of the Politburo. In practice the Politburo determined composition of the Central Committee. No Party Congress would fail to approve the Politburo's nominees, nor will it those of the now styled Presidium. Pending a Party Congress the Central

Committee fills its own and Presidium vacancies. The October, 1952, Congress enlarged the Committee to 125 full members and 110 alternates.

The Soviet State Constitution has been in flux much of the time since its mere blueprint status of 1917. While formal structure has been maintained, emphasis has definitely shifted. With Stalin in the saddle, authority no longer moved upward from the Party Congress, represented by the Central Committee, but downward from the Politburo, originally the auxiliary organ, so to say. This full reversal of the original concept for the party structure was meant to objectify the political doctrine described as "democratic centralization" in Communist terms.

To that brain of the Soviet government, the party furnishes the body if that simile is able to serve as an illustration of a form of rule so alien to anything known in the West. In this context, the down-the-line party organizations serve as handmaids and watchdogs of the Politburo, both inside of the party and relative to the administrative apparatus called euphemistically "government," which is no more than an indispensable instrument of the party and an ever suspect one. Taken as a whole, the party appears as its own guard. If any deviation outcrops, major or minor, the fact or even suspicion of it moves up the line from spying nuclei on guard in every factory, every labor union, collective, office building, press room, dwelling unit, university faculty, or what have you.

The party is formed by "cells," plausibly called the "primary organs of the party." They exist in numerous compartments—on each local spot and along the way higher up. Along with the higher echelons they are strung to the Secretariat of the party in Moscow, whose executive was Stalin until a few years ago. They are subordinated also, directly or indirectly, to the Political Police. The interlocking agencies operate like a nervous system. Outbound from center, they have as precise and minute effect as when the will of a man orders the movements of his toes and fingers. Inbound, they set up a service of intelligence and dutiful response approaching perfection.

This machinery directed by the Politburo dominated and guided the "government," reduced thus to the exercise of administrative functions in the strict sense of the term, but stripped of the political connotations which Westerners are wont to believe inherent in the concept of "government." The only change is in name from Politburo to Presidium.

No minority attempt to exercise intra-party freedom has occurred since the most ruthless of several party purges raged the four years from 1934 to 1938. This followed the assassination of Politburo member Kirov. Expulsion then overtook a fourth of the membership and over half of the enrolled candidates. The attending executions cut down member generals, ex-ambassadors, and other formerly high placed government officials, including "old Bolshevists" who were one-time top figures in the party, the government and the Comintern. Yezhov, chief of the Political Police who had to execute his predecessor Yagoda, before it ended paid the supreme penalty himself.

Elections a la Soviet

The anatomy of the Soviet governmental structure and the elective system abundantly guarantee power staying where it is—in the Politburo or its equivalent. The right of franchise extends broadly to all citizens who have reached the age of eighteen years irrespective of race, nationality, sex, religion, education, domicile, social origin, property status or past activities, excepting only insane persons and those whose sentences for crime included loss of electoral rights. The constitution bravely declares suffrage to be universal, equal and direct by secret ballot.

The elective machinery that delivers all power unfailingly into the hands of about three percent of the population goes into gear at the early stage of nominations in the respective election districts. The party units, trade unions, cooperatives, collective farms, youth and cultural societies may nominate. The representatives present their candidates in a joint meeting of all concerned. Upheld hands signify approval or rejection. If more than one nominee wins approval, an elimination process behind the scenes streamlines the slate down to a single ticket. If in isolated cases competition at the polls has taken place, it was indulged after the several candidates had passed screening tests by party officers. Numerous non-party nominees secure approval and election. The ratio lessens on the way up the hierarchical levels, until in the Supreme Soviet of the Union it drops down to one in five. At election time the heat turned on for all-out voting puts the unchallenged ticket over by as high as 99% of all voting eligibles, according to official reports.

The blanket appropriation of power by the Party Central Committee—old Politburo minority—comes with election of the State Presidium* and the appointment of the Council of Ministers by the Supreme Soviet. It turns out that membership in these two top-flight policy-making and executive organs has corresponded almost man for man with that in the Party Central Committee and Politburo. No nonparty member has yet graced either body. Both in effect are projections of the Politburo handful that selects them. Here within the conclave resides the will of the Russia that we face. Mere analyses of the written constitution and of the party code will never lead to understanding the actual working of the political machinery, or of the distribution of power in government. The case is of the kind about which Zinoviev, President of the Third International, wrote as to relations between it and the Soviet government: "It would be laughable to question . . . who is subject and who is object. They are foundation and roof of one building."

The State Structure

The U.S.S.R. apparatus for administration of government, created by the

---

* To be distinguished from the newly styled Presidium in the party organization.

party, is perforce its creature. An approach to saying so appears in Article 126 of the present Constitution. This sets the party politically apart and above. The text reads: ". . . the most active and politically conscious citizens in the ranks of the working class and other sections of the working people unite in the Communist party of the Soviet Union (Bolsheviks), which is the vanguard of the working people in their struggle to strengthen and develop the Socialist system, and is the leading core of all organizations of the working people, both public and state."

The Communist party masters laid down the original Constitution and fashioned all its revisions. The last fifteen words quoted above are not there casually. They state the fact in Communist terms that the clutch of over-all party power meshes into the gears of government and drives the entire apparatus. The governmental functions naturally parallel those of governments the world over. But viewed as a power unity, it differs from them by complete dependency on the party centralized authority. It is thoroughly bureaucratic. However novel, the combination works well enough for Mussolini and Hitler to have tried to infringe the patent.

Pyramid in conception, the structure of government rises from local soviets (councils) up through the successive geographical unit soviets of counties, towns, cities, regions, provinces and constituent republics to the Supreme Soviet of dual houses. "The Soviet of the Union" consists of deputies elected by districts, each embracing 300,000 of population. The network of political divisions, from Constituent Republics down to the lesser national areas, contribute respective quotas of deputies to compose the parallel "Soviet of Nationalities." The two chambers have equal status. With respect to legislation the Supreme Soviet actions amount to no more than ratifying nominations and measures brought in from appropriate administration sources that previously received their directives from the Party Central Committee—Politburo set. In fourteen years, as the constitution requires, the Supreme Soviet has been in session twice annually for something like a week each time. No defeat of any single proposal, no adverse committee report, no speech in opposition, nor any less vote than one of unanimity has attended procedures in either house. Budgets and tax rises even go through with lusty applause.

The Supreme Soviet exercises what (Politburo aside) would be three great prerogatives of power—the election of its own Presidium of thirty-two members; the appointment of a Council of Ministers (formerly Peoples' Commissars) numbering up to fifty members; and election for five year terms of nearly 100 judges and associates to the Supreme Soviet system of courts.

The powers ascribed to the Presidium tower above those of the two last named organs. Together the trio reflect the unique character of this Soviet structure in that it wraps up in a three-in-one package what orthodox political science distinguishes as legislative, executive and judicial branches. All functions of the Supreme Soviet descend to the Presidium between the normal one week sessions held twice a year. These added to those prescribed as the Presidium's own functions make a list truly impressive—all the authorizations of governmental powers there are in fact. It convenes the Supreme Soviet itself and, with that in adjournment, interprets the laws of the USSR, amends and revokes them, or issues new ones by edict. At all seasons it employs and releases Ministers; annuls at will decisions and orders of their Council; appoints and removes the high command of the armed forces; proclaims a state of war; orders mobilization and declares martial law; appoints and recalls diplomatic personnel; ratifies and denounces international treaties. Nothing thus is lacking to effect legislation; to interpret, amend or revoke laws; or to execute them.

The constitution styles the Council of Ministers "the government of the USSR." In terms of the outer political world, it is something more than a cabinet, yet less than Executive Branch, inasmuch as the Presidium overhead may intervene at any point. And from the party powerhouse outside, the one guiding Politburo will is regnant. Appending from the Supreme Soviet and Presidium and accountable to them, the Council (with its limitations) takes administrative measures binding throughout the Soviet Union; activates the national economic plan, state budget, credit and monetary system; adopts and applies means for maintaining public order, state security and the rights of citizens; directs the general organization of the armed forces; exercises guidance in relationships with foreign countries; and sets up any special agencies required in economic, cultural and security affairs. The term "security" ever evokes recognition of the ubiquitous M.V.D. and its police agents virtually outside the law, who infiltrate every other Ministry from its heart center out to the tiniest of the capillaries.

The outreaching multiple arms of the Council of Ministers vary in numbers around fifty. Their roster highlights the fact that all-out Socialism takes over direct management of the whole range of a people's life. This Communist built apparatus starts with administration in those standard areas with which democratic governments have familiarity—Foreign Affairs, Defense, Internal Security, Currency, the Post, Justice, Communications and Transport (in Europe). Beyond the exercise of those accustomed functions, this Socialist state owns and, through its Ministries operates, to name a few, such industries as aircraft, automobiles, agricultural stocks, machinery, medical supplies, oil, rubber, coal, iron and steel, chemicals, power and the list runs on. This government management, moreover, is comprehensive from overhead to the last detail of production, distribution, financing, employment, wages and prices to the consumers. The new administration moves toward consolidating related Ministries, apparently to tighten control.

Mention of the far-reaching monopolistic Foreign Trade Ministry suggests but one of the wide departures in government a la Soviet from the pattern of free enterprise. It has been called the most colossal cartel in the world. The other trading nations rightly view with deep concern the spread of Soviet economic domination across new territory. "Amtorg" takes over Russian business there. It possesses with a vengeance the power of negotiation characteristic of the representatives of monopolized interests. Another free market disappears from the international scene.

Two-fifths of the Ministries in the Council have the designation Union-Republican. They provide the liaison between All-Union administration and that of the sixteen constituent Republics, each of which has its own complete state apparatus of the All-Union pattern. The functions allocated to the organs of the Republics are minimal compared with those left to the states by the American constitution. Certain of the Ministries of the Republics function simply as projections of their opposites in the Union. These have responsibilities within the All-Russian armed forces, foreign affairs, state security, justice, and finance areas. Other Republic Ministries as named below deal with industries in the economy employing the mass population and determining living levels. Such categories embrace meat, fish, dairy products, groceries, textiles, building materials, light industry, public health, higher education. The structure as drafted suggests administrative decentralization. Some degree of it does exist, though control from the center never relaxes.

The measure of autonomy enjoyed within the Republics is that remaining after All-Union direct operations have taken over Five Year Planning, Budget, Taxation, the Monetary and Credit System, Transport, Communications, Foreign Policy, Defense, Armed Forces, including the sleepless Political Police. To insure conformity down into the affairs of private life, a Republic Ministry takes on administration in such areas as education, health, marriage and the family only after the Union organs have laid down basic policies and programs in no little detail. For example, in education the Party Central Committee and the USSR Council of Ministers carry through to the point of issuing jointly explicit directives concerning courses, textbooks, and teaching methods for elementary and secondary schools.

At the apex the Presidium insures legislative and executive regularity down to grass roots with its power to nullify any law, edict or order of a Republic's Supreme Soviet, Presidium, or Council of Ministers. The final guarantee of conformity stems from the party whose founders rejected the principle of federalism. That repository of ultimate power at the center binds every member to the party line, and the party line streamlines all government policies and programs and attends upon their execution.

Five Year Planning

The planned economy in itself holds all of life in a viselike grip, whether private or official, by its all-embracing scope and details. Over-ruling authority stems from the main lines having been laid down jointly by the Party Central Committee and the Council of Ministers. The State Planning Commission (Gosplan) takes over, implemented with some forty odd specializing divisions, each with several sections and thousands of expert, statistical and other personnel. This body shapes a five year program to the mandatory pattern out of meticulous data gathered countrywide.

The country gets a look at the trial plan, then sends it back with a mixture of acceptances and proposed revisions. Gosplan proceeds to perfect the draft for execution across the Union's length and breadth. It is issued jointly by Party Central Committee and Council of Ministers—the standard procedure when the stakes are high. The entire population now address themselves to fulfilment of the complex project, impressive in high production figures for coal, ores, steel, oil, chemicals, power, transport, autos, planes, ships, tanks, trucks, guns, tractors, machinery, and the miscellany wherewith they shall be housed, fed, clothed, taught, recreated, nursed and policed.

Four of the plans have run their course since 1928. World War II lengthened Number Four in years. These instruments of centralized power regulate the cost of government for every political unit large and small. That alone precludes essential governing independence all down the line. As for individual economic freedoms, the plan specifies the payrolls and wage funds industry by industry, apportioned finally to each area and to this and that factory. Each collective farm has production and delivery quotas handed it for grains, livestock and their products, forage stuff, capped by labor hours per adult. And the check-up system gives quotas the force of commands. This is Socialism Supreme across the board. Comparatively, what the most fearsome see of it in the American sky cannot yet be discerned "as large as a man's hand." It could appear just about that size in today's Britain. The disciples of Marx and Lenin call what we have "anarchy," but we prefer it.

The Will and World Mission

The mighty potentials of the Union of Soviet Socialist Republics have been committed to and are being wielded by this extra-legal yet de facto will the world mission of revolutionary communism. And for action outside the Soviet realm, peaceful penetration and deployment of force blend in a composite strategy. The two coalesce in a given situation at a point in time romantically styled "the historic moment." This may arrive in a stated country when there prevails among the people widespread discontent with their lot, confusion over public events, and loss of confidence in ruling politics. The states of mind may follow an exhausting war, especially if lost; or attend a ruinous economic depression; or rise out of long suppressed resentment against social injustices in the land.

24

This formula for revolution prescribes that in such situations a small disciplined party of Communists, who know where they want to go, will make large promises of release and relief and be ready to do what dying is necessary, can manipulate the masses to permit the fractional minority seizure of power. Lenin managed to do this rather handily in 1917 in Russia when his party of enrolled members numbered fewer than 200,000.

The strategists prefer that these coups prove practicable more or less painlessly in country A, then in B, and so on where and when conditions ripen into opportunity. They believe it essential enough to prepare intensively for it. Simultaneously with the advent of Soviet power, they created the Third International (Comintern) to found, officer and measurably implement a Communist party in more than sixty countries. A school for party workers in Moscow distributed free scholarships over the world to approved candidates. Funds flowed freely from Moscow sources in direct aid of revolutionary enterprises abroad. As types, the Red International of Labor Unions supplied money for organizational work among British miners and subsidized the party newspaper in London.

Coincident with the General Strike for British workers set up in 1926, foreign residents in Moscow saw both Comintern and Soviet officials fairly agog over the event as immediate precursor of the revolution in Great Britain. They actually moved to put important Russian personnel on the ground to give it impulse and direction. The strike collapsed before the emissaries could leave the revolutionary fatherland. A gathering of O.G.P.U. men for Radek to summon to new duty did not have time to materialize.

French occupation of the Ruhr in 1923 prompted them to encourage the German party to capitalize on the tensions. For financing the eruptive putsch, $10,000,000 worth of marks were put on deposit at the Deutsche Bank in Berlin. Discussion waxed warm in the Russian party leadership on whether to intervene militarily. It went so far as to consider asking the Polish government to permit Red Army troops to cross its territory to reach the German scene, where Communist rule had been actually set up in Saxony. Such support did not materialize and the eruption subsided. At a high point in the German-Soviet relations, Stalin (then a comparatively obscure Commissar) flared out to an interviewing Berlin correspondent on what would be done "when we get to Germany."

Bedsedovsky, once highly placed in the Tokyo Soviet Embassy, after renouncing allegiance, published among his revelations that the Moscow Politburo directed the Commissar of Finance in 1925 to make available $25,000,000 to the Comintern's agents in China. The Council of People's Commissars secretly ratified the grant which materialized in the form of munitions, aircraft and military instructors.

"The University for the Laboring Masses of China in the Name of Sun Yat Sen," established in Moscow in 1925, had 800 Chinese students gratuitously enrolled in 1928 for training in revolutionary leadership. General Chang, who presented the Korean case for the Communist Peiping government before the United Nations Security Council in 1951 is one of the products. He conducted himself as an authentic Bolshevist "graduate" specimen. Therein a shuddering fact stands out. The true breed gets reproduced in other peoples by insemination from another national stock. Training does the rest.

Thus sparked from Moscow, Communist revolutionary striking forces have become rooted in most of the political divisions of the world—minors as well as majors. Yet, from 1917 to 1940, efforts made in this conspiratorial manner yielded no new Communist states. A few of importance narrowly missed that subversion. Seizure of power became imminent in Italy, Germany, Spain and China. The dictator systems led by Mussolini, Hitler, Franco and Chiang-Kai-shek set them back for the time.

Nothing daunted, the driving minds pressed the offensive on every front with recent successes. China has been captured, parts of the continent too, and the rest besieged. The system continues to maintain a supply of chosen, taught and seasoned top leaders for foreign situations. At the close of World War II, the French Thorez, Italian Togliatti, Croatian Tito, Bulgarian Dimitrov, Rumanian Ann Pauker, Polish Berman and Bierut reappeared in their homelands to take over operations in the crisis period. They did so, coached on thirty years of Russian party techniques of social warfare to employ, and with the prestige and experience of four star generals.

The Communist underground across the free world conceals a network of like trained agents, if of lesser stature. The schools to prepare home propagandists and agents for infiltration of other lands enroll trainees in six figures and budget their outlays in millions of dollars annually. A reliable resident of the Ethiopian capital reports the known presence of over 100 Communist agents in even that remote and backward country.

Historic Moments Arrive

From the days of its outbreak, World War II opened the way to actually combine "historic moment" techniques with the Red Army's prophetic role in world revolution. The fate of eastern Poland demonstrates well the liaison at work. On August 23, 1939, Hitler signed with Moscow the pact that green-lighted him for his attack on the Poles nine days later. It had given Der Fuhrer assurance that the Soviets would keep their hands off. The Germans broke Polish military power in less than four weeks. Thereupon Moscow threw down its nonaggression treaty with the Poles and drove its armies across 47 percent of their territory.

With Soviet troops on the scene the Polish Communist party went into action. At least 1,000,000 of the population were loaded into box and cattle

26

cars to be strewn over the Arctic and desert spaces of European and Asiatic Russia. The significance of that operation lies in who were the million— the more experienced and accepted leaders of the Poles in government, industry, commerce, finance, education and general culture. The deportations amputated the population's leadership.

Implementing the economic revolution briskly ensued with industry, major channels of distribution, banks, mines, forests, foreign trade nationalized. A regime of political police superseded the heretofore existing order for personal security and justice. The police administered whatever form and measure of terror proved needful to paralyze resistance or drive it under cover. The educational system yielded content and program to dictatorial directions. These placed under control all formal channels of intelligence to the brain, whether press, radio, cinema, stage, school or literature. For the mind of a nation bound to Communist rule must be emptied of all ideas and knowledge that do not accord with communism and be refilled with strictly prescribed contents.

This lending of Soviet armed strength to the indigenous parties of "struggling proletarians" since 1940 has established and entrenched totalitarian satellite regimes in Albania, Bulgaria, Estonia, Jugoslavia (since broken away from the Kremlin) Latvia, Lithuania, Rumania, Eastern Germany and Poland, retailored by Soviet annexation of the already severed eastern populations and by Polish occupation of Silesia, Pomerania, and such of East Prussia as remains after the Soviet has helped itself to key positions. Save in the three small Baltic States, the U.S.S.R.'s single handed interventions were made *after* Stalin in 1945 signed with Churchill and Roosevelt their joint communique at the close of the fateful Yalta Conference, pledging cooperative measures for economic recovery and political reorganization of these identical peoples along democratic lines.

Known Armed Strength and Capacity

The armed land forces that the Soviet Union has in hand, equipped and otherwise readied for combat, far exceed those of all the western powers within striking distance, whether for offense or defense, in Europe or Asia. Current outside estimates vary. As early as July 31, 1951, the Economist (London) used the figure of 215 divisions (40 antiair and artillery), put out by the British Under Secretary for War. An equal number of trained reserves available to the Soviet power, if called up, would very quickly build up the land army equal in strength to the one that halted the Wehrmacht before the essential German objectives were reached. Soviet tactics in war demand and use up the soldiery in mass. Red generals put expendability at figures shocking to Western Commanders. Accordingly, the latter reckon that their forces, armed and deployed for resistance, do not call for equal numbers to counter the other's armed strength.

The present supply of tanks, guns and munitions of all description, trucks and other means of transport should certainly exceed the U.S.S.R. stores of 1940. Productive capacities now in operation materially outclass those at the time of the German invasion. What the present potentials are is suggested by the levels that the Soviet industrial performance attained in that war. The huge totals of Lend-Lease material that arrived from Britain and North America amounted to only one-tenth of what it took to resist and drive out Hitler's legions. The rest came out of Soviet factories.

Expert Solomon Schwartz, in the New York Times (March 16, 1952), rated the Soviet Union militarily "stronger now than ever before in peace-time." But not strong enough, the Kremlin considers, judged by the later budget allocations adopted by the Supreme Soviet. Our State Department estimates that one-half of them go to increase military strength in labeled armament brackets. The supporting outputs of steel, oil and tools, already in forced production, also will rise to peak heights. Moreover, the precious steel tonnage will be applied where it counts most for power. The 1951 allotment for automobiles, refrigerators and washing machines did not measure over two percent. Even plants for tractors, trucks and locomotives yield to the pressure for sterner stuff. This disposition contrasts sharply with U. S. production policy that continues to apply strategic metals heavily to civilian uses.

That disparity in costs insures more manpower and firepower flowing from equal expenditures there than here needs to enter into comparative reckonings. Oil excepted, the Soviet Union has in its earth the known basic minerals to maintain the militarily spurred up gait indefinitely. The needed amount of labor abounds there, unequal to the West in skills, yet good enough, unless in limited lines of specialization. The Russian peoples' living can be pinched to whatever degree financing requires, by the "butters" being sacrificed for "guns." Soviet steel workers cannot strike to maintain their living standard against rising costs, nor private owners lock them out. No farm lobby exists to keep up parity prices on the cotton, grain, meat and dairy products of the collective farm peasants. People hover at the brink of subnormal physical ability to produce. But the Kremlin seems to gauge the point where lowered consumption would render acute the risk of some form of revolt. The mass Soviet population emerged from the war economy in 1945 with sharply de-pleted energy that took the first few succeeding years of peace to restore in some degree impossible to know conclusively.

One wonders whether our present day, easy going Americans, living in such comfort as never before, have the "staying powers" to face up to the long, gruelling, costly struggle against the Malenkov-Molotov-Beria forces and their Communist cohorts inside and outside the Soviet Union. We have exhibited such powers in the past. At the very birth of the nation, our colonial fathers, mothers and sons stood steady for eight long years for freedom's sake. Our Southern people fought in the long years of struggle between the states, to emerge exhausted but undaunted, taking up the unspectacular task of rebuilding their economy that has held their patience and effort for a full half century.

These reflections are not without pertinence in the present day appraisal of what we must do to face Russia successfully. Great sacrifices now of money, of living standards, of some lives may well prove the means of preventing that third world war from which none will emerge victorious. The masters in the Kremlin will make careful note of our every move, appraising our staying powers, our will to go all the way in support of freedom's cause. They will be quick to take advantage of our failures now as they have done heretofore. They will not miss the evidence of our success either, and in that lies one hope of such amelioration of conditions as will make a viable peace possible—a truce at least.

The Russian masses will have no respite. Two Five Year Plans after the current one remain of the three prescribed by Stalin in 1946 to double coal production, up that for pig iron one-and-a-half times, for steel one-and-a-third and oil 70 percent. More plans than two will be required to match the present going rates of the NATO aggregate of mines and mills. And the recent Party Congress raised the sights commensurately. Posited against 142.3 million metric tons of crude steel output of the West in 1950, the Soviet Union and satellites figure stood at 35 million tons. By 1952 Russia and her satellites were producing steel at an annual rate of approximately 43 million tons. The contrasting totals for crude oil were 459.1 million tons and 46. But by 1952 Russia had stepped up oil production to 60 million tons. For primary aluminum 1,206,500 metric tons for the NATO nations as compared to 192,500 for the Soviet bloc.

The Soviet Air Force holds fewer advantages over the West than its Army counterpart, despite numerical superiority in planes. The estimated 19,000 military aircraft at present, and 1,000 more in monthly production if used on the offensive in Europe, the Middle East and Far Orient would give those areas a very bad time. One need look no farther to account for the neutralism and cautious foreign policy towards Moscow with which diplomacy out of Washington has to deal.

The national leaders of peoples within a few hundred miles of the Soviet bases can reckon on no such measure of security by reason of distance as the major industrial centers of the United States enjoy. The nearest Russian bombers based across the Bering Strait from Alaska should be able in force to operate reliably not much farther inland than our Pacific Northwest states and return. Those East Siberian bases moreover present serious problems of weather and supply. The next nearer ones are hundreds of miles into the interior parts and so are their biggest North American targets.

Little of the Soviet land, with its far-flung industries, lies beyond the round trip range of western air bases from which atom loaded bombers can take off in armada strength. Aircraft carriers interlace the intervening seas with bombers aboard two to six hours distant from key Soviet industrial regions. Hanson W. Baldwin thinks "our (atomic) stockpile is numbered probably in a small four figures, the Russians probably—but not certainly—in two." Our longest range bombers and refueling facilities have undergone tests that assure ability to strike even from American home bases. Other bases girt the globe from Greenland, Iceland, across western Europe, North Africa and into the Middle East, then crosses to the Okinawas, Japan and Korea. American flying and operating personnel equal twice the Soviet number. They brook no inferiority man for man in any capacity.

If, as believed, the Russian navy has cruisers, battleships and carriers reckoned in all on the fingers of two hands, but with more building, Soviet surface power afloat can do little more than act on the defensive outside the Black and Baltic Seas. These it should dominate. Brassey's 1951 "Armed Forces Year Book" puts the Kremlin's submarine strength numerically at 500 vessels built and building—ten times the German undersea craft at the time of Pearl Harbor. Yet the wide spread of four oceans and their great arms to be policed blunts a lot the formidability of this array. Notwithstanding, such power could work havoc on many enemy ships, cargoes and crews.

If American foreign policy, as now, keeps Europe central on its diplomatic board, relative armed strengths on the continent have special significance. The opposing issues over Germany could become acute enough to bring on armed conflict. The stake of both sides is monumentally high. Western Europe cannot be secured against Communist armed aggression from the East without the German West. On the other side, without embracing all Germany, Soviet Russia would be logistically off balance in a fully armed Europe, both in manpower and other military potentials. With all of NATO in the calculation, the total industrial superiority of the West over the Soviet Union and its European satellites is three to one. If Moscow expects to alter the disadvantage, time is running out, despite the mounting strength of the Soviet potential.

British Under Secretary of War Wyatt in 1952, located twenty-two fully equipped Soviet divisions in East Germany, eighteen of them armored. For them NATO has matching strength west of the Elbe. At the moment nothing imminent rises on the scene. No reports come out of a buildup of Soviet forces on their own western frontier as if getting poised to attack. Yet it will be recalled that Stalin delayed major assaults against the Germans until they could be delivered with great mass force. The deduction may be drawn that a move now, precipitating a third world war, would be done in overwhelming force for quick success before the ultimately superior weight of opposing resources could interpose. Evidence of such preparation has not been manifest. Meanwhile, the top diplomats of East and West counter

30

wits and bid for German favor. Their over-all armaments mount, nowhere more accelerated than among the European satellites.

Satellite Contributions

Armed forces under virtual, where not immediate, Soviet command grow in the European satellites. The London Polish weekly, "Wiadomosci," prints impressive figures and descriptions of these, provided by Kazimierz Smorgorzevski, highly expert on Eastern and Central Continental affairs. As of July 1, 1951, the total of divisions in the six states stood at fifty-five, to be brought to seventy during 1952.

Poland with sixteen divisions and four to go illustrates the well balanced dispositions. Four are mechanized, four motorized, four new ones will be. Standard Soviet equipment rules, not of the heavier type whether tanks, guns, or planes, although Czech Skoda makes heavy ones. The countries themselves all produce according to capacity and the nature of their industries. Soviet officials and directors on the ground control production.

Soviet Marshal Rokossovsky is Polish Chief Commander and Minister of Defense. His four regional army chiefs are Red Army generals. Soviet officers appear numerously in both Defense Ministry and General Staff. Czechoslovakia's eight divisions, being upped to twelve, have for superior command the "Soviet Military Mission" in Prague under Colonel-General Gusev. He has on his staff down the line six Soviet generals, thirty colonels, seventy majors and several hundred of lesser officer rank. The appointments to high command provide like security in Hungary, Rumania, Bulgaria, and Albania (a Vice-Admiral here). At the very top the Soviet Union Ministry of the Armed Forces has a "Bureau of Allied Armies" directed by the very able Marshal A. M. Bulganin with Party Presidium status.

On the further precautionary side elite "home forces," after the Soviet pattern, make up a significant portion of the establishment in each of the satellites, designed apparently for protection of the regime itself whether in peace or war, to include perhaps dealing with defections at the front. Overall recruitment for the Services starts at the age of twenty. The periods vary from two to three years depending on the branch entered.

Arming of East Germany also has disturbing proportions, sparked by a Soviet Military Mission on the ground—with one Red Army general at the head with two Soviet general assistants. One of the latter is from the Political Police branch of the Moscow Ministry of the Interior. The German police chiefs take orders here. Three former German Army generals work on the military job projected to reach thirteen divisions. Eleven officer schools now have the training of something like 1,000 students. The measure of security risk inhering in these forces is open to questioning. Hanson W.

Baldwin reported from Frankfurt last October that about 380 members of the so-called German police forces deserted to the Berlin west sectors in September.

Assorted Accessories and Affinities

The power that the Kremlin wields in the still free world extends to some degree over every continent. It takes varied forms, some directed by the single guiding intelligence and authority, others may be ascribed to polar attraction or even spontaneity. The strength that nearly drew Western Europe into the Soviet embrace and still threatens there, issues largely from controls exercised within the trade unions. Communist "cells" embedded in nonparty social organizations undertake in all countries to direct the decisions and actions of large, often unsuspecting mass bodies. Majorities prove unnecessary to successful operation. Ten per cent they reckon sufficient for swinging the ninety. Lenin sought only "sympathy of the masses" as requisite to victory. He called his early dynamic, revolutionary sheet "Iskra" (the Spark) enough to touch off conflagration.

The Russian party fathers under his leadership launched their worldwide infiltration program in 1918. Ten years later operations had proceeded from blueprint to the Comintern's successful spawning of parties and going auxiliary concerns in all twenty-five countries of Europe, ten in the Americas, three in the Far East and in South Africa, Australia, Indonesia and India. Current events uncover how widely and deeply penetration has gone among all ages, both sexes, every race, the underprivileged and rich, relief agencies, the schools and universities, scientific societies, departments of state, armies, shipping, workers in the factories, even into the secrecies of atom bomb production.

These useful human elements outside the Soviet Union and the recognized Communist parties in some half a hundred other countries, have been styled by themselves or others the Underground, Fifth Columns, Fronts, Fellow-Travelers or Parlor Pinks (the tail of the Comet). Authentic data on categories one and two fatten the files of security and defense agencies over the world. In well-established vigorous government systems their factual strength is known probably with near approximation. Measures have been devised presumably to deal with them in crises. In France and Italy serious subversive attempts originating in these quarters must be anticipated if the cold war turns hot. Thus far both governments have proved ready when their Communists got boisterous. Such hazards would scale down to a low point, we trust, in Anglo-Saxon, Netherlands and Scandinavian countries to obstructive tactics in strategic industries, the great ports and rail centers, along with more hidden sabotage, some explosions and the like. The F.B.I. and Scotland Yard could be expected to pull in their nets of marked and suspect cases overnight.

Pinks and fellow travelers have thriven in the free open spaces of the democracies. The assortment at large can be exonerated from the charge of traitorous intent. Along with the willing and convinced, can be recognized the deluded but pure in heart, the grossly deceived and trapped, and the hopelessly gullible. Some unknown number doubtless assume one of the roles to mask the work of authentic Reds, such as have been exposed infiltrated into government, industry, education and other strategic spots of influence. The rank and file of them furnish the Fronts membership and financial support. These often take up causes of merit but get steered by the wily "cell" members inside to the advantage of the latter's own distinctly revolutionary aims and the international finaglings of Moscow.

Rising during the decade antecedent to 1940, in and out of Fronts, they had field days during the period of World War II. A tact armistice for the duration suspended political, economic and ideological conflict between Allies. Each power sought to get as much all-out fighting as possible from the others. Goodwill needed to be maintained even if at a high price. And some shocking prices were paid. Our Ambassador Davies gave us from Moscow intimations of a kindly, domestic Stalin with small children climbing into his fatherly embrace. A film derived from his "Mission to Moscow" book later met public denunciation by twenty eminent scholars as a travesty on history. Silences covered up crimes of genocide proportions. From ignorance, or on the advice of government (surely informed itself), much of the press and most of the columnists and commentators by-passed the brutal exile of those million Poles from the leadership of their people for half of them to die out in the Soviet wastes or at slave labor.

Professional and other fellow-travelers organized the chorus of demands for an Allied Second Front in Western Europe against the timing of the American and British General Staffs. In other like ventures Moscow exerted its pressures in the United States through the spokesmen of more than seventy nationwide organizations and national committees, which, according to the New Leader (Socialist), October 12, 1946, had been "founded and conquered or . . . predominantly influenced" by the Kremlin's international Communist machine.

Withal the international stage was set for the post-war entry of all inter-allied statesmen, who would address themselves to the building of a One World Society of people and states living in peace and plenty with one another. Millions of our citizens' dollars had been poured forth in good faith for legitimate Russian private relief. Government billions had gone into lend-lease and UNRRA appropriations of immense import. The San Francisco Conference enacted the first somewhat heartening scene.

It was stated that the United Nations Charter represented honest purpose on the part of all the participating states to try bridging the difference between two social orders sufficiently to keep them functioning peacefully toward each other, in short, coexistence. The chiefs of communism, however, elected to throw away the world of good will fairly won by the brave and powerful Soviet armies and the great Russian people, and to go all out for global revolution and power. The wonder is that so much surprise should be voiced at this action since that program has been from the beginning the purpose of their party.

GREAT UNANSWERED QUESTIONS

How Much Enduring Loyalty?

Now a crucial question. Can the Soviet Union soldiery and civilian population be depended upon in all-out war if called on by the Kremlin to do so? For how long? And with what heart? The pros and cons yield no answer on which inquiring minds can rest, or cabinets and general staffs firmly base their actions. To state a few of the main ones will mark off the wide range of uncertainties existing both in the East and West.

A certain natural mental attitude to resist attack is presumed. The land of Russian Slavs has been much coveted, raided and ravished for centuries. To defend it when threatened and to recover it when lost, long generations of the past have demonstrated great loyalty, courage, capacity to sacrifice and they have met with great successes. Those forebears have handed down historic deposits of fighting qualities to successive generations.

Thirty-seven years of Soviet warnings in and out of season about exposure of the Russian State to a ring of capitalistic powers harboring evil purposes proved to have at least this validity that over the period from 1918 into the early twenties armed foreign interventions struck at the Young Red regime on its perimeter from the north, east, south, and west. And they were all thrown back. In any new crisis, the government's near monopoly of means to reach the popular mind can be trusted to present it as one calling for a last ditch defense of the Fatherland.

Yet it must be recalled that large elements in the army and civil population did hail the Germans as liberators in 1941. Too much can be drawn too easily from that precedent. The treatment given the people a la Nazi brought sudden disillusionment to the wavering Russians and threw them back into Stalin's arms for stonewall resistance to the invaders. The Allies compounded the shock. They forced many thousands of German held prisoners of war and slave laborers, who elected not to be repatriated, to entrain back to Communist rule at American and British gun and bayonet points. The Yalta agreements had included one pledging each power to return to their homeland the others' citizens found in its jurisdiction.

All this does not wholly gainsay possibilities that understandingly good treatment of civilian population and prisoners by another foreign army, once on the ground, would not somewhat counter such memories and fears. Media like the Voice of America from the outside should be able to effect in the mind of many Russians some identification of the free world's policies with their own aspirations for liberty and the good life. Nothing of this character would be more determining than what the propaganda of the

West can establish as its honest thought about territorial unity, national freedom and personal security.

The generally depressive material and social circumstances of Soviet life could very well be disposing new elements of the army and people toward defection to a foreign army once within reach. However, in 1941 the masses on the whole held steady when levels of life prevailed as low as now. And in the long war years they reached tragically sacrificial depths. Incertitude on this loyalty matter constitutes risk for either Soviet Russia or any of its enemies provoking war.

Life in the Soviet Union does go hard currently for the "toiling masses," in Communist parlance "flower of the revolution," from which many petals have been heedlessly bruised. "Toil" is the word, forty-eight hours a week, largely enforced and at low pay in terms of what the wage will buy. In labor time the average Soviet worker pays for his family's essential foods at from one to twelve times the scale of his Belgian opposite. Comparison with the American worker's consumption widens the spread into a chasm.

Only an elite in the party, certain professions and superior industrial brackets have meat or fish oftener than once a week. Sugar, butter, eggs are on the distinctively luxury list, milk scarcely less so, but for children available in limited portions. It takes twenty-eight hours of pay of the average worker to buy a kilo of coffee (2.2 pounds). The current Five Year Plan has scaled shoes manufacture to barely more than a pair per person a year. Purchase of a pair of the least expensive men's leather shoes uses up the pay of a week and a half, even after the April, 1953, price reduction. For a man's good suit of clothes he will work about eighteen weeks. Periodic reductions in the price of consumers' goods reflect not so much their sudden "abundance" as the politcal need to ease the strain under which the masses must live and work.

Fully one-half the employees in industry are women—in coal mining, steel mills, on the docks, too, and in large numbers. They must become employed to live. Mere housewifery does not entitle a woman to housing privileges and other necessities of existence. The average wage of one person will not support a household.

Rent and utility charges appear low, yet not actually so for the facilities they provide. The housing regulations make 8¼ square meters a legal minimum space per person. For a family of four this translates into 16 x 22 feet. The figures exclude bath, toilet and kitchen since several families on an apartment corridor will share a unit of those respective facilities. Millions of Soviet dwellers have no more than those 352 square feet to call home in which to eat, sleep, sit, sew, read and enjoy the social amenities of family life.

Still, striking out against life on that level probably occurs to few, for it is not disturbingly new and slowly improves. Much of urban labor had shabby housing before the revolution—less sanitary most of it. Black bread, the coarser vegetables, nourishing soups, kasha of buckwheat or millet, occasional meat or fish made up then as now the routine unsweetened, butterless, monotonous procession of meals. It is a safe prediction that the present Soviet generation will not revolt against economic living conditions. No one under forty years old remembers anything better, and few even of the older generation among the urban masses.

Then a time of plenty awaits just ahead, so the government promises. When the factories are built and efficient, the collective farms all mechanized and contented peasants render them more fully productive, there will be surpluses. These will not go to enrich capitalistic mill owners and landlords, but into better housing, more perozki, bleenies, blouses, shoes and skirts. Blueprints of a complete apartment with bath for every worker's family have been on the boards for the duration of all the Five Year Plans.

It does not follow that these promises of the party chiefs are made insincerely. Rather they will go on to project more Five Year Plans, ballooning heavy industry, before they allow consumer goods to take the necessary priority in production quotas to ease up much on day to day existence. Roughly forty per cent of the national income is plowed in to heavy industry and other capital enterprises. Armament projects take the heavier tolls. As one planner put it, "we take butter and make bricks."

Meanwhile, so the official story runs, the workers under capitalism have so much less of life's satisfactions. Pravda (Truth), great party organ, two years ago reported eighty percent of the population in the United States to be living "below subsistence level." During the last war Minister of Labor Shvernik issued a statement explaining the necessity of stepping up work week hours. To cushion the blow he told the over-all Trade Union Council that the new forty-eight hour week in Russia would be still "the shortest in the world." He explained that ten to twelve hours a day were enforced in capitalist countries. Moreover there workers were denied a weekly rest as "all Sundays and holidays had been abolished." Information to neutralize this false line filters in almost negligibly. Years ago Stalin told Harry Hopkins the barriers to travel, news and other intercommunications would stay up till the living level inside approximated that outside. Their lowering on occasion to special groups such as touring newspaper men may be done to serve a particular purpose in the over-all strategy. But it would be most unwise to take this as prima facie evidence of an "about face" in social intercourse between Russia and the western capitalist world.

Again consider how hardships remain easier to take where much better living standards never prevailed except as now for the privileged few. Besides, Soviet workers have certain post-revolution gains for consolation and encouragement. Such have come in the areas of social welfare and security.

37

Before Communist rule, the worker bore in his own body the hazards of his existence in respect to accidents, sickness, old age, unemployment. The constitution stipulates "the right to work." The by-laws make work obligatory. He receives free hospitalization and medical care, enjoys vacations on pay. The wife in a maternity period gets appreciable time off on pay before and following childbirth. There are more school privileges for his children within reach than formerly. While the home is crowded "the parks of culture and rest," sports fields, and club rooms in some plants provide outlets for relaxation. Though meagre, a pension ensues in the years when unemployable.

Even when they are heard, promises from the outer world of the liberty and bounty that genuine democracy holds in store have scant objective reality in the minds of these humble millions. It was democratic parties of native Russians that brought about the revolution proper which gave them promise of all the gains they now count and vastly more, and freedom withal. A Bolshevist coup d'etat robbed them of the opportunity to try the experiment in democratic living. Among the middle-aged and elders, that dream perchance survives in faded glory.

The Communists had never attained position in the Duma where the liberals turned rising heat and pressure on the autocracy. To the Constituent Assembly, freely chosen after the Tsar's abdication, the electorate returned one Communist to three of their opponents. Lenin, with his "Red Guard" revolutionists, dissolved the Assembly after a single sitting. The act sealed the passing of all power from the democratic provisional government, stemming legally from the Duma, to the self-constituted Soviets.

Any one then age six is now over forty. What surrounds him and manages his life from cradle to burial is *normal,* as natural as the Volga, winter and summer, the Kremlin wall and the sky above. A discouragingly inert weight of ignorance, shored up with party indoctrination, overlays the mass mind of Soviet millions. And something like eternal patience marks the Russian character.

While history shows that Russian character can be oppressed beyond what seems human endurance, to get much farther now than wishful thinking about revolt in the U.S.S.R. against the system, one needs first to prospect for leadership of it. The Cheka, "sword of the revolution" as the early Bolsheviks called it, at the outset destroyed open and potential resisters on the ground. The Cheka's successors have kept new ones drained off into the slave labor camps. Other first class figures fled the country. Age has overtaken most of those emigres not already claimed by death. Outside organizations of the old and new escapees do not appear impressive to date. Beyond sheer physical survival they have first to struggle for surface unity among themselves.

38

The Peasant Hard Core

True, the peasants have given the party unremitting headaches. Their prerevolution individual and village holdings amounted to eighty per cent of the cultivated land. The Bolsheviks told them in 1917 to take over the landlords' estates except certain very large ones reserved for State operated farms. This they did. Forced collectivization from 1929 on, compounded with nationalization, divested them of title and of free working rights to both their own and the newly seized holdings. Then much went wrong: grain seizures by the State, forced sale of products at low price, high cost and great scarcity of farm machinery and consumer goods; many scores of peasant revolts; and the retaliatory killing of Commissars in 1927-28.

The collective farm regimen claims by far the major part of the members' work time, organizes them into working brigades, assigns each the labor to be performed, and by book accounting of hours, nature and quality of performance apportions the returns in cash and kind at a season's end. Peasant resistance to all this rocked the countryside. But communism in power does not wage class war with feather dusters. The process of collectivization that got into full swing in 1929 "liquidated" a million of the best farmer families, confiscated their private possessions and drove them from the land. These dispossessed made up the first mass intake of labor camp inmates.

Ukranian peasants on a large scale in 1932-33 sabotaged production by seeding, tending and reaping badly. The state lifted out its quota as from a full crop regardless. The grain export that year was 1,500,000 tons. W. H. Chamberlin called what followed "a state organized famine." Several million persons died of ensuing starvation and diseases incident to malnutrition in the winter of 1933-34. The experience broke open resistance but resentment smoulders. Hunger for land ownership and its independent cultivation remains. Whether it was abated or whetted by the private usufruct of a tiny parcel subsequently granted each household has not been established. It was a concession wrung from the state in a period of acute tension and attending sabotage.

Significantly, these small patches became at once the most fruitful ground in the Soviet Union. The families contrive to extract disproportionate yields from that soil, and supplementary returns in poultry, dairy and meat products. The upturn in meat and dairy production from the lags that ruled after collectivization dates from the transfer of the fragmentary plots into private hands. Government organs ever protest the way the private allotments have of growing bigger. Vigilance at the top relaxed during the war. The widespread accretions that came about evoked a thunderous shakedown of holdings and of grassroots administrators. Some regional heads fell as well. In fact, it took a Politburo member to get the score back to normalcy where it still refuses to stay.

Statewide collectivization, inescapable under socialism, has justified itself to government by two results. Mechanization, fertilizers and better seed selection and distribution measurably step up the total of production and fit what is raised into the planned economy. Government gets first-hand control of it all. With production up a possible one-third since collectivization, state procurements have swollen fourfold. An editor in the Ministry of Agriculture boasts: "The highest proportion of marketings in the world." In respect to farm deliveries to the state, the term "First Commandment" has come into official use. The state enforces this sale to itself of a large share of producion at miserly low prices to be processed for sale to urban consumers at huge profit. The write-up from expropriated cereals at the farm to bread loaves has been estimated as high as eight hundred per cent. Financing of the great industrial construction program thus weighs heavily on the backs of the peasants. They feel and resent it.

Increasingly direct party control of the collectives has been necessary to cope with that seemingly irresistible growth of the small individual land allotments at the expense of the general patrimony, concealment of crop and livestock returns, illegal sale of produce in the market, and widespread "thievery." Returned German war prisoners and civilian draftees used on the collective farms, and fortunate enough to be repatriated, bring out first hand reports to the same effect.

How Resistance Fares

The M.V.D. political police have ears and eyes for rural and urban scene alike. The outfit embraces well over one million personnel, including its own army with artillery and air force. The army unit came into existence for interior purposes in 1926 when peasant discontents seemed getting out of hand. In the decade that followed, this force grew to a fully equipped complement some 300,000 strong. The whole million in M.V.D. rate as the best housed, fed, and clothed forces in the Union.

As far back as 1937 when information was freer, the annual budget of this state police combination equaled $375,000,000. Hitler's S. S. instrument of power partially paralleled this Soviet installation, yet only part way for M.V.D. forces stand guard on all frontiers. Government of the strategic regions also reposes in these mailed fists. Its sleuths infiltrate the domestic population at every angle on all levels from topside down into each local party segmentation, armed unit, factory, office, collective farm and apartment and more than possibly one's own family.

No citizen can have absent from his mind the probability that he is tailed by a spy; accordingly that any act, expression, or mood critical of the ruling order will be reported to the political police system. He knows that the power lodged there can add him without trial to the slave camp millions.

These administrators of terror, moreover, have an incentive for recruiting additions to the camp populations. They actually operate under compulsion to produce heavy quotas for the industries worked by the mass of political prisoners and so need the labor.

No reliable estimates of the number of workers so impounded employ figures less than 5,000,000. Some range up to three times that number made by serious probers into that darkest section of the Soviet labor world. On completion of the single Baltic-White Sea canal over 50,000 camp workers on the job were released and hailed for good performance. The number who died on that Arctic project is not a matter of public record. If more numerous than the survivors, the score would not be unusual, for the Soviet press gave out the figure of 250,000 being used on that project at one time.

Where under or outside the over-all police dragnet will subversive purpose, talent and courage hide, much less organize to effect action? Beyond question capacities for revolt reside in Russian character. They are human beings. Not a few souls, most resolute and wary, do escape, driven to take the desperate chance at deliverance. Many tens of thousands of Russians held prisoners of war by the Germans and those whom the Nazis conscripted for labor in the German factories, once out, refused to return home in 1945. Others expatriated themselves by coming out ahead of the retreating German armies. These considerable quotas by their presence and testimony warrant some presumption that in case of war anti-Soviet armed forces on the ground would precipitate no small defection of people from the Moscow government. No more than fragmentary evidence exists that it would assume proportions of a popular uprising. There would probably be no response at all to a returning German invading army because of the bitter experience of the early 1940's.

The Soviet army suffers only slight defection from the East occupation forces into the American and British Zones—rarely of officer status. Opportunity to do so exists in that area. As many as fifteen to twenty thousand German civilians get over in given months. Other thousands of civilians of the varied satellites escape their Iron Curtain borders.

Shortly before the start of the second World War something got afoot in the highest Red army ranks that issued in the trial and execution of the brilliant Tukachevsky and most of the other top generals, together with colonels, and majors down the line. It is not beyond peradventure, of course, that some such rupture could recur and involve important cadres of the armed forces.

Significantly, the Politburo has been kept closed to professional military figures other than the lifelong Communist Voroshilov, who is not a really trained soldier nor a successful one. Stalin's Generalissimo title came by edict, also Zhdanov's citation after his role as Commissar in the successful defense of Leningrad. A political Commissar, responsible to the top Party Control Office, shadows every officer of rank for security purposes.

The Ultimate Testing Ground

If the character of a people influences in determining ways their ultimate action in situations, the reservoir of character in the Russian nature may not be overlooked for qualities that will outlive, outthink, and sometime overcome oppressors. In Soviet Russia, government and the power behind it do not reflect the national character. A ruling system, essentially an alien "graft on the native stock" envelopes the population. Intelligent foreigners, whose Russian contacts have been long, close and responsible, uniformly identify this basic Slav material as first rate human stuff. They will be found subscribing substantially to the findings and assay of George Kennan, our thoroughly grounded former Ambassador in Moscow. On the firm prediction that there exists such a thing as national greatness, he eloquently testifies:

"... the Russian people possess it in high degree. They are a people whose progress out of darkness and squalor has been a painful one, marked by enormous sufferings and punctuated by heart-rending setbacks. Nowhere on the face of the globe has the tiny flame of faith in the dignity and charity of man flickered more precariously under the winds that tore at it. Yet it has never gone out; it is not extinguished today even in the heart of the Russian land, and whoever studies the struggle of the Russian spirit through the ages can only bare his head in admiration before those Russian peoples who kept it alight through their sacrifices and sufferings."

Consistently, this competent American, widely trusted regarding Soviet affairs, does not abandon faith that resident forces may resolve ultimately what appears an impasse today. In the last chapter of Kennan's "American Diplomacy," he thus rules out despair:

"Superficial evidences would not seem to leave much room for hope that the changes we would wish to see in the attitudes and practice of government in Moscow could come about without violent breaks in the continuity of power, that is, without the overthrow of the system ... Stranger things have happened, though not much stranger ... We should allow here for all possibilities, and should exclude none ... in all our dealings with Russian political factors, including both that which is in power and those which are in opposition. And if it should turn out to be the will of fate that freedom should come to Russia by erosion from despotism rather than by the violent upthrust of liberty, let us be able to say that our policy was such as to favor it, and that we did not hamper it by preconception or impatience or despair."

Speculation on the chance of change by counter-revolution rather than "freedom coming by erosion" has some historic support for the premise that, when tyranny imposes unbearable conditions, resistance erupts. A European journalist of distinction, stationed for years on the Soviet scene where he was able to get insights, builds up a case for antigovernment tendencies that must eventuate in widespread fear and provocative hate at least. He places the arbitrary lawlessness of Kremlin rule above any measure of physical suffering as a paramount force for inducing rebellion.

Misrule first finds expression most sharply in the amoral methods of the secret police. They alone who have lived in such circumstances can imagine the psychological effect on the individual of unendurable permanent anxiety, with fear raised to the intensity of unrelieved, continued toothache. It is present with equal strength in the muzhik of a far gubernia and the party Commissar. Whom to trust? When the midnight knock at the door? A Kravchenko now and then "chooses" freedom. The Gromykos and Maliks stand by divested of even the shadow of independence or security. Ever present apprehensions deepen the chasm between their minds and those of the West. Mrs. Roosevelt says of her U.N. work that she has never broken through a Soviet official's mind to human ground. Workers in the refugee organizations find that the displaced persons lately out of the police state need assurance that they do not have to lie to live.

One of the most seasoned and penetrating of foreign correspondents thinks few stranger things have taken place in history than the XXth century Russians "flying wholesale and heedlessly sometime into any light that shines into their ignoble dungeon." This diagnostician believes that America will do wisely to amplify the "Voice" speaking to Russians of Western concern for their deliverance, not so much by praising American privileges, performance and wealth as by giving a clear outline of Russia's future, as viewed by the governments of the Atlantic Alliance and as confirmed by concrete pledges. Among these, the most important will be the stand taken by the United States in these directions.

Predictions of action by a people so circumstanced necessarily expose their author to a certain charge of irresponsibility. But it is imperative to keep in mind that the psychological factor is the most potent, not only in leaders but in the mental process of the mass. To make clear to ourselves the distinction between the Russian people and their Communist rulers and to keep that distinction clear in our attitude and conduct is of importance. To bring the Russian people to a realization of our friendship toward them is a diplomatic "must" in the solution of our common problems.

Concerning Satellite Dependability

Calculations vary about the bedrock gains to Soviet power by accession of the European satellite states. They must be reckoned important economically. Silesian coal and iron, great enterprises like the Czech Skoda armament works, the skills of East Zone German artisans, add precious assets to the Soviet economy. All major production lines have been woven into the Soviet system by nationalization or joint ownership split 50-50 with the master power with all the breaks in its favor. Moscow pays the Poles for their superior hard coal about one-tenth its worth on the European market. The Czechs receive nothing for the product of the uranian mines in their territory worked in complete secrecy under direct Russian management, and much of it by forced imprisoned labor. The propaganda for consumption of the exploited nationals represents such concessions as rewards for the Red army's service in liberating their lands from German rule.

Period planning forces the pace of heavy industry from the Baltic to the Balkans. As in the Soviet Union, this stress to produce capital goods reduces supplies for domestic consumption. The populations resent the imposed lowered living standards, pressed down further by draining off industrial and agricultural products for export to the Soviet east. The subservient press lashes out monotonously at slackers and saboteurs in factories and within the very Communist national administrations. The political police pack the culprits off to homegrown labor camps or to corresponding Soviet reception centers. Successions of top Communists hang their predecessors.

Soviet military forces, on satellite ground, and in control of all other arms two-thirds of the way across Europe, have enormous significance. Thereby 100,000,000 non-Russians have their freedom of national action suppressed. The best of Europe's bread basket has been attached. The area contains the four chief rivers that carry the heavy traffic of eastern and central Europe north and south—the Vistula, Oder, Elbe and lower Danube. The roll of its cities includes Riga, Warsaw, Krakow, Stettin, Danzig, Berlin, Leipzig, Frankfurt-on-Oder, Dresden, Chemnitz, Prague, Vienna, Bratislava, Budapest, Bucharest, Sofia. Its northern waterfront circles enough of the Baltic to reduce that sea to a Russian lake.

Historically, when the Turkish tide ebbed out of the Balkans, British, French, German and Austrian teamwork prevented the Tsars from gaining supremacy of influence on the Balkan peninsula. Their successor got astride all of it except Greece. Tito later gave him a fall in Jugoslavia. Still the Russian measure of strength in the Balkans has no precedent in their history. Malenkov's tanks, guns and bombers mount behind the Iron Curtain at the door of Hamburg, along the Elbe, and farther west to the Harz mountains. His positions include the famed Erzgebirge fortress range, and Linz on the middle Danube. The Albanian shore lines on the Adriatic and Ionian seas afford his submarines shelter, if not a base, at a strategic Mediterranean gateway.

Soviet generals have ultimate, where not direct, command of all satellite armed forces slated to reach fifty-five divisions in 1952. Belief that numerous nationals will not take their orders if the chips are down has some good foundations. The Poles regained independence after having imperial Austria, Russia and Germany on their backs for 125 years. Polish distrust and hatred of Russians has the seasoned quality of a millenium. How contemporary experience in Poland could be expected to mollify feelings is not readily apparent. Soviet wartime and postwar policy toward Poland has been one deliberately calculated to eviscerate that nation. It will have been proved effective if the living Poles can overlook the August, 1939, pact with Hitler; the rape of nearly half their territory; the murder of the flower of Polish officer prisoners of war by thousands in the Katyn forest and elsewhere; the studied betrayal of Warsaw's last gallant uprising against the Germans; the liquidation of their heroic underground fighting units; and the thrusting of national renegades to power over them by fraud, terror and bayonets.

The Czechs in 1914 seized upon the chance to free themselves from three centuries of Austrian Hapsburg oppressions when the Vienna government mobilized their conscripts to fight Tsarist Russia. They went over to the Russians by regiments to the steps of their national martial music. After the 1948 Communist coup, the strength of Czech civilian leadership escaped the executioners. They are in exile organized for redemptive action. They will lay more than even odds that the spirit of the 1914 Legionaires would in eventualities render any Czechoslovak army a Soviet liability at least. The men in the Kremlin cannot be without misgivings on such scores as this. The recurring purges within the highest of the Czech Party itself exposes instability in the very ruling quarter. The symptoms may well serve to check further aggression on the continent until a generation of training in communism gives better prospects of loyalty.

The Southern Slavs too will belie their sturdy forebears if they are found prostrate before the Soviet overlords at the end of the day. Tito has already spoken up for the Croats, Serbs, Slovenes and Montenegrins. The Bulgars have yet to validate the witness of Stoyan Pribichevich:

"The Balkanite has survived all who oppressed him. The haughty Roman has long since gone, and become unrecognizable, but the Greek he despised is still here, and on the very same spot. Hordes of aggressors have vanished into nothing, empires have fallen to dust, but the tiny Slav nations tenaciously cling to the soil they occupied more than a thousand years ago."

Which Way the Middle East

One would like to establish factually that there are resident in the Middle East (across the whole Asian mainland indeed) assured adequate reservoirs of resistance to communism's advance ready to be identified with the defensive efforts of the free world. The course of current events affords much less than a bright prospect of any such early realization. The West is in general retreat before the surges of nationalism in Asia. Western policies of the past have conditioned that super-strategic area to the advantage of Soviet operations in two important respects.

Country after country demands self-mastery in its own house and over its own possessions. With these aspirations Communist international agencies directed from Moscow have long been associated. If they did not plant the ideas, they have assiduously tilled and watered them. Hence Soviet credits now stand over against grievous discredits earned over the long period of rule and exploitation by Western imperialism.

To be sure, if once communized, experience elsewhere indicates that they would find the Soviet brand of nationalism sold them amounting merely to a dialectical stage on the way to Communist revolution and the ruling arm of Moscow. But in the current political heat and tensions, what that rule, sparked by the Kremlin, would entail on people and present rulers waits for consideration. For now as in Iran and Egypt, slogans ring out the changes on "away with the imperial foreign masters." These are pay-offs on Western imperialism and the strategy that the Comintern has pursued from Moscow for thirty-four years. Against such consistency of purpose and procedure, Western powers flounder in opportunistic diplomacy, as often as otherwise in jealous conflict with each other.

Prevailing injustices and other evils that characterize the social order in most of these lands provide a second condition favoring Communist penetration. In the better situations the social structure is feudal with the historic disparities of position and wealth between the thin ruling level and a subject people. In some more involved situations, such as Iran, the extremes appear of a fractional, rich, land-owning, state-bolstered, corrupt and possessive minority fattened off the masses who are poverty stricken, ignorant, diseased and lacking leadership from within their own group, except, as a sincere reformer might appear from among the owning class, or as the Communists who aspire to control might succeed in taking that role. The little better conditioned Egyptian masses appear to have found promise at the hands of General Neguib and his surrounding younger military men. Trust the Communists to seek his undoing as they did successfully the revolutionary provisional government in Russia in 1917. Happily these Communists of Egyptian breed are not numerous. This will not deter the Moscow comrades from plotting difficulties along with Neguib's enemies.

The Red seed has been freely sown. Enough has sprouted to give the politicos and their sponsors pause. They join in the aroused public upsurge of nationalism to resecure if possible their own shaken base of support. Soviet agents with skills and experience thread themselves through the populace, to conduct the flame of revolt to the entire political and economic structure when the "historic moment" comes. Moslem revulsion against Communist atheism may prove equal to confounding the strategy. It is a ground for hope because organic and not improvised or exotic. To date Islam has presented a stiffer front to communism than the Christian world. The long overdue radical land reform moves of the Shah, Mossedegh and the successor government to the deposed Farouk serve notice that in Iran and Egypt the hour is striking for break-up of the status quo. Will democracy succeed in taking over?

The United States does not have handily wrapped up proposals about the way forward acceptable to authorities playing up to rampant nationalism. We have a large stake in Middle East oil alone. This smacks of the hated, doomed imperialism, however fair the terms offered and accepted for concessions. Communist propaganda steps up the charge of exploitation to the nth degree. Vishinsky calls for all foreign armed forces to be drawn out of Egypt. We associate our power with that of Great Britain to insure the safety of the Suez Canal. Washington presses Iran and Downing Street for an oil settlement within all bounds of reason. Our best ally does not wholly relish it. Mossedegh and the Iranians balk because our Treasury refuses to prop up the exchequer with nine figure loans.

If the good offices of Washington as a friendly power concerned with just and peaceful settlements of Arab-Moslem-Asian issues go begging, the case is one of paying off for our Administration's weight thrown in on Israel's side in critical decisions against Arabian "rights" in Palestine. The result is Moslem faith in America brought to an all time low from India to Gibraltar. Dispossession of hundreds of thousands of Arabs of their lands and homes rankles unabated. Hence there is ominous consistency in Arab alignments in the United Nations whenever voting or abstention will score against an American led Western bloc. Warranted or not, the effect weights the scales of influence Sovietwise.

On Matching Strength with Strength

Whenever a "change of pace" was executed by the Kremlin under Stalin, or as now perhaps by his successors, it has been taken by some immediately to mean an abandonment of the long purpose to communize the world. There follow promptings to reduce our military strength, stretch out our defense buildup, resort once again to a dependence on Soviet goodwill to keep the peace and allow us a calming respite from our fears. We will do well to keep the vigil on Soviet military policies and practices now, if and when this occurs. For matching strength with strength is one reality that the Kremlin masters take into account. Unless and until Soviet military programs alter in tangible ways that show clearly steps toward disarmament, it would be the height of folly to lower our guard at the first sound of pacific phrases on the lips of the new Kremlin leadership or of the echoing spokesmen in China.

The West has found no rational alternative to rugged rearmament in the face of Soviet operating power policies since 1945, when Moscow showed no intention to parallel the other Allies in their rapid disarming. For its purposes the Soviet government maintained armed strength sufficient to over-run the continent of Europe, the Middle East and the mainland of East Asia, although no military establishment of threatening proportions or purpose existed on or near Soviet frontiers. It threw back into the faces of Great Britain and the United States offers to join in making permanent the demilitarized status of Germany and Japan. The Soviet representatives in the several United Nations organs have consistently blocked agreements that the free world was ready to enter into for regularizing armament levels across the map on an equity basis with assurance of effective inspection. Forswearing Stalin's pledge to Churchill and Roosevelt at Yalta to co-operate mutually in the peaceful political and economic rehabilitation of Eastern, Central and Balkan Europe, the Kremlin, with its armies on the ground or posted at the frontiers, established Communist minorities in power in six countries and now fosters their arming to the teeth under what amounts to Soviet high command.

Communist operations in Asia, inspired and supported behind the scenes from Moscow, reflect no more peaceful intentions. Resistance to the guerillas in Malaya draw heavily on British arms. Viet Minh besets the French in Indo-China, while divisions of Moscow's Mao lurk across the border and Russian made equipment pours in. Chinese manpower, thrown at United Nations forces in Korea, poses grim possibilities in the Far East. These summon the nations still free to be strong, whether for negotiations or for sterner eventualities.

With such happy hunting grounds at hand over which to range, Soviet aggressive moves, within any period of profitable speculation, appear likely to follow the time worn pattern of piecemeal operations (however thinly disguised), rather than to risk everything in total war. Rashness did not characterize the old Politburo in foreign policies. The members are no Hitlers. Dating from the proclaimed Truman doctrine, they have not hazarded a third world war while the Marshall Plan, Atlantic Pact and NATO have whittled down their earlier power advantages.

The gates of opportunity had been wide open to them, with destruction visited on the German and Japanese military machines; the West comparatively demobilized; and the shaken political structure of Europe awaiting only a putsch to bring much of it down in collapse. Still the latent power of the West, its overbalancing industrial capacities and the larger atomic stockpile, could well have been the over-ruling considerations with prudent men. But they have moved on the double-quick to outpace Western rearmament. Stalin would give another interview on the conditional co-existence of Communist and capitalistic powers, and with his colleagues (now the succession) strain to draw Western Germany into their orbit, as if permanently to unbalance the rest of Europe with their weight of power.

However "inevitably" war may loom to the master minds of world revolution, no timetable for the onset has ever been hinted. The record indicates that none exists. When blocked off from a course, they patiently turn moderate, and even reasonable for a time. In 1917 Lenin believed the other states of Europe ripe for falling into the lap of communism. He moved into appropriate action. One of the early appropriations of his government was a sizeable one to finance the exterior agencies of revolt. The funds, ironically enough, were committed to the Commissar for Foreign Affairs to dispense—one Leon Trotsky.

Lenin was mistaken. Europe stabilized. When his program met successful resistance in every continental state, his emissaries applied to the same threatened chancelleries for recognition and acceptance into the family of nations of the Soviet Socialist Republic as a good neighbor. When granted, endurable inter-relations followed for a quarter century. In no way had the reversal signified abandonment of world revolution or the use of force to accelerate it. As Lenin, who taught "retreat to avert disaster," would say, the action was "recoil to leap farther" in the next world crisis. The aftermaths of World War II provided just that crisis. It all argues convincingly for the build up and maintenance of barriers all around the place, even if we are on the eve of another feint at retreat.

To be sure foreign diplomats did not live happily with their Soviet opposites after the recognition and nonaggression pacts. Anthony Eden knew that well when, with post-World War II negotiations under way, he promised the House of Commons in the business of international settlements "plenty of difficulties, plenty of disappointments and much deception." Even so, Mr. Churchill and all contemporaries, practiced in the civilized code of diplomatic procedures, were due to be baffled, when not infuriated, in encounters with the mentality and amorality of orthodox Communists. Statesmanship had never met their kind in national authority well entrenched in power. Down through diplomatic history honesty has been freely imposed upon by falsification, trickery and default as a technique of action. Here a great power resorts to all of them.

Membership in the League of Nations did not restrain the U.S.S.R. from assault on little Finland. It risked and met the penalty of expulsion. So, today, abatement of the "cold war" by a Soviet state incalculably stronger may appear as a final bid for peace. But Kremlin policy behind the scenes will continue to stem from an "enemy" concept of the democratic, free enterprise world. That mind-set has shown no deviation since its blunt expression at Genoa in 1922 in a top-flight conference of World War I

Allies met to gear Germany once more into continental affairs of state. There the hitherto excluded Soviet government had a representative sitting by invitation in the person of Gregory Chicherin, Commissar for Foreign Affairs. A man of the press suggested to him mediation of the issues between the Moscow regime and the Geneva system. Chicherin emphatically responded that two opposing worlds here faced one another and that between them no neutral nation, position or party existed.

And tragic consequences will again follow for the free world, as they did after 1918, whenever custodians of its interests tend to overlook the awesome fact that Moscow's aim is fixed, and by now is so deeply embedded in its power practice as to render a reversal of its methods and principles extremely difficult if not virtually impossible for the regime. Gibbon's words prove all too true in the instance that regimes are maintained by employing the same means for their security by which they were founded. Hostility against the traditional regimes has been the Soviet's life source from the start.

AS SEEN AND EXPOUNDED BY OTHERS

A School for "Understanding" Soviet Russia

Starting with the end of World War II hostilities, the flouting self-exposures by the Kremlin of its nature and objective deflated numerous of the Fronts and discouraged most of those who before could be termed innocent fellow-travellers. Unawareness of Soviet design was no longer possible in most intelligent quarters.

Despite the continuing impact of Moscow's self-revelations, a school of thinking that would have us understand Soviet Russia *its way* bravely carries on. This school still advances the claim that true knowledge of the system, its creators, objectives and achievements will yield enough appreciation of their nature and worth in themselves to pave the way here and now for friendly, cooperative, international relations. Proponents of this view, some influentially placed, reach the public with it by way of the press, radio, and classroom and books. They forswear Communist affiliations and purposes. The disclaimers will and should be accepted in good faith.

Standard techniques employed would persuade mankind that the institution hidden behind the Iron Curtain is, when all is said, nobly undertaking furtherance of human welfare as its true objective, has already delivered the Soviet population far along the way to the good life, and can be trusted to act with good will and peaceful intent toward all understanding peoples and their governments. The working kit takes over for adaptation a familiar assortment of padded claims, half truths, falsifications, even condonement of crimes, and other impositions on an illy informed and confiding public —all so characteristic of official Soviet propaganda.

What most affronts and confounds rational understanding are the aberrations of interpretation that if accepted would make the Russian Communist system appear something other than the founders meant it to become, and that the present directing heads in their time now strive with unswerving will and energy to effect—a conspiracy of destruction against free men, free enterprise and free peoples across the world. In the language of Dorothy Thompson, they are dedicated to "tearing up the very roots of Western Civilization and Culture."

A Sample School Book

One account that has obtained wide currency is the book "Behind Soviet Power" * by Dr. Jerome Davis. Some source made a copy available to each

* The Reader's Press, Inc., N. Y. 1946.

of 22,000 Methodist ministers through the good offices of the Board of Foreign Missions of that Communion. The space of another book would be necessary to explain all the manipulations of material. Some examples illustrate how it can be done.

In respect to relations with the United States, Soviet policy received implied vindication from this author. He invokes thirty-odd cases in which the course pursued by our government, press and public toward the other power and people has been wrong. The critical citations begin with refusal at the time to recognize as valid the Bolshevik seizure of power in Petrograd in 1917, and to go along from the start with that regime as the legitimate Russian government. For this omission America gets assessed with much of the responsibility for the sequence of events that led to World War II. The charges of major and minor misdealings accumulate right up to the date of the book's authoring, climaxed by the warning that they mark out the path to World War III.

The book urges that President Truman should go to Moscow to talk with Stalin. Secretary of State Marshall should have approved another Big Four meeting of Foreign Ministers, ignoring existence of the United Nations then dealing with the very matters of controversy. Atom bomb controls should be set up acceptable to Moscow. Our treasury should make a $6,000,000,000 loan to speed up Soviet recovery. Our bid for Pacific bases under United Nations trusteeship justified the Kremlin in seizing outright those within its reach and asking for more. Russian power on the Turkish Straits would be of a piece with American unitary possession and administration of the Panama Canal. Our two ocean navy and the proposal to continue military conscription provoked Stalin's bristling 1946 May Day speech.

So, logically enough, Dr. Davis assesses Washington with the duty of taking initiatives to break the impasses. Yet he gives the many advances taken here and rebuffed there no recognition. From early World War II days this nation acting bipartisanly broke with historic policy to project friendly cooperative undertakings on international levels. From San Francisco on, Moscow first remained unresponsive, later met overtures with abuse, and pressed the satellite states into the practice of aloofness if not hostility.

The attacking author does not venture to explain the absence of Soviet representation in the democratically instituted organizations for international cooperation in the fields of labor, trade, food, health, commercial aviation, finance, European recovery, education, science and culture.

An American could, it would seem, recognize that the series of proposals made to Moscow and rejected had the virtue of good faith at least. The list is impressive: a common guarantee against German and Japanese

52

aggression over a twenty-five-year term, or forty if it suited better; a share in the Marshall Plan for Europe's recovery; readiness to rest effective atom energy production and use with the United Nations; collaboration in peace treaty making with Japan; reciprocal air service between the two countries; student, scientific and publication exchanges. However, Soviet spokesmen translate them into machinations of economic imperialism, war mongering, and lust for world domination. And in "Behind Soviet Power" the charges are unchallenged.

Black becomes White — Nearly

Any such presumptive interpreter of some major Kremlin interior revolutionary measures meets dilemmas. He gets called upon to choose between denunciation of them and the smoothing over of callous national crimes with abject extenuations. They are such as cannot be ignored. Dr. Davis impales himself on the latter horn, and drinks the dregs of palliatives. He drips mercy and forgiveness on world known proceedings that have shocked most of normal humanity. After the assassination of Kirov in 1934, with which a dozen persons or at most a few scores may have shared some guilt, between 70,000 and 80,000 executions shed blood over the land. Without reference to this instance or any other concrete case of systematic terror, the author proffers the consolation that "fanaticism, hysteria and bureaucracy inevitably cause some injustices."

Similarly, the drive for farm collectivization that destroyed a million of the most industrious and successful farm families passes inspection with the lofty judgment: "it was a harsh policy and many died." The anti-religious campaign, readers are told, "never went to the lengths that many people imagine," yet "possibly 1,000 priests and forty bishops died in the Revolution." There could have been cited also, from the chief of the concentration camps administration that as of May 20, 1936, there were 9,126 ministers of various confessions in the camps (not including those in exile). The Commissariat of Internal Affairs whose political agents enforced the Kremlin's will in these wholesale processes of extermination, according to the Davis version of its business, handles security police work "similar to our F.B.I."

Like light touches dispose of major violences to the basic political conceptions of democracy. The interventions that turned free nations into puppet states constitute "a protective tolerance to new ways in economic and social organization." In fear of attack from the West, the East regime "believes in having as much land as possible" between itself and the capitalists. "A freedom of speech which any country might envy" exists "within the limits of the system," (if anything factual survives this double talk).

The old imperial annexations come in for blessing evidently for "much of the land Russia has been getting back was what formerly belonged to her." Heightened gratification should be penned over that reclamation of the three small Baltic peoples. The returning conquerors this time insure themselves permanence of possession by the creeping genocide of Estonians, Latvians and Lithuanians, and their replacement by imported Slavs, Buriats and other Mongols. Silesian and Sudeten homes emptied of Germans are receiving similar alien refills.

Whether or not Soviet diplomacy can be trusted, Dr. Davis answers in full affirmative, despite the nearly unbroken record of past betrayals of trust. Molotov certified to the Supreme Soviet in 1939 that the pacts with the Baltic states were "based on mutual respect for the political, social and economic structure of the contracting parties," and that all charges of Sovietizing them were "nonsense." Within a year all three had been made Republics of the Soviet Union. Further entangled, the author of "Behind Soviet Power," challenges successful proof "that Russia did not live up to the Yalta agreement on Poland." American Ambassador Lane had proof enough to resign as the most emphatic protest he could make over what Moscow was doing to that three party joint agreement made in 1945, "to assist the peoples liberated from the domination of Nazi Germany . . . to solve *by democratic means* their pressing political and economic problems."

The British and American chiefs had committed the execution of their pledge of cooperative assistance to their respective Foreign Ambassadors acting with the Moscow Foreign Minister. Yet, throughout the area, the Kremlin agents uniformly proceeded to take unilateral determining action. The independence of Rumania first went down the drain. Molotov so flouted the two colleagues over Poland that they discontinued meetings. Cables of protest from Washington and London to Moscow multiplied. The "free and strong Poland" that Stalin once unctuously invoked had been doomed in fact from 1939 when Molotov boasted to the Supreme Soviet: "One swift blow, first by the German army and then by the Red army, and nothing was left of that ugly offspring of the Versailles Treaty." The reduction of Albania, Hungary and Bulgaria to puppet status paralleled that of Poland in time and method. Yugoslavia too, but Tito cut the strings.

Finally Czechoslovakia, where the last hope died that people of a lesser power having in its government Communists, obedient to the Kremlin, would be permitted to retain any essential freedom. Stalin assured Benes in person, as Molotov had the Balts, that the integrity of Czech political, economic and cultural institutions stood apart from their mutual assistance contract and would be respected. As a piece of Kremlin "respect," the same Stalin categorically demanded that the Communist Gottwald, Czechoslovak Prime Minister, revoke the decision of his Cabinet to be represented in the Paris meeting of Europeans to consider the Marshall Plan offer. And he was obeyed.

In respect to propaganda guilt, Dr. Davis thus wraps us up together with our defamers: "Both Russia and America have been placing sinister interpretations on each other." "Falsehoods, forgeries and black propaganda about Russia circulated all over the world." So far as his record reads, this seems to even up the score. "Habitual exaggeration of the evils of the West" out of Moscow, he curiously times as "before the war."

An instructor in this kind of understanding of Soviet Russia must somehow validate swollen pretensions and claims, and play down liabilities that get assessed against the system. Those that just inconveniently will not stay down in this account were taken personally to Stalin who pleads his own case adroitly. No cross examination. Case dismissed. The procedure might bring to an irreverent mind the refrain of a revivalist hymn, "A little talk with Jesus makes it right, all right."

The matter of labor discipline came up in one of the Stalin-Davis talks. The Communist Chief was found to believe "more genuine economic democracy" prevailed there than in the West where under capitalism "the workers regard their factory as a prison." The reporter Davis submits nothing to deflate the preposterous conceit. A puncture or two here may perhaps suffice. Since 1938, a labor book carried by every Soviet worker informs the employer of an applicant's education, trade experience, job record, his moves and the causes, and any bonus earnings. The engaging employer retains the book for the duration of the job. Hiring elsewhere is impossible without the book and the record up to date. Unrepealed wartime decrees nail wage and salaried employees of all categories in their places. Transfers rest solely with employing heads. Leave taking on one's own brings down prison penalties. Absenteeism is penalized by up to six months of corrective labor (the slave camp). Under Supreme Court ruling, twenty minutes late adds up to decamping. Trud, official labor organ, as late as September, 1948, voiced the government's pressure for stricter enforcements. American workers in their "prison" are remote anyway from such harsh labor laws.

To return to the stalwart peasantry, on one of the little talks with Stalin this same writer picked up the fiction that they received their land from the ruling party and were grateful to it. He subsequently uses the claim as factual, though the peasants owned eighty per cent of the land in 1917 through personal or village holdings, only to lose to the state all title by constitutional nationalization. He relays to his public the further Stalin falsification that in collectivization the rurals got what they wanted. Then why the known fact that several millions of them met death in opposing it? That the peasants on the way into the collectives slaughtered for private uses a fourth of the country's cattle, a third of the sheep and half the swine? Surely not in enthusiasm over their dispossession.

In his "Complete Works" (1949), Stalin afforded in striking terms the difference between his utterances to comrades and what he puts into the pipeline for "understanders." In Volume II he presented "Savings within the nation as the sole means for financing Russian industrialization," and proceeded to locate the sources of wealth as "first the working class, which creates the real values and operates industry; and second the peasantry: the peasantry pays to the State not only the direct and indirect taxes, but *overpays* through high prices for industrial articles. Furthermore, the peasantry *does not receive the entire price* for the agricultural products. * * * It is a kind of tribute, kind of overtax which we must take temporarily." (The italics are Stalin's.)

While still out on the land, "Behind Soviet Power" tenders another contribution to "understanding." This shows up in what may be called stepping up a factual minnow into a whale of generalization. The account presents a community of 400 peasants that voluntarily organized themselves into a collective in 1929. The picture of prosperity, buildings and living accessories would fit into the frame of one of Iowa's favored counties. The director figured out on a cash basis for this reporter the farm's values accruing to the members in a year, including home consumption. It averaged about $11,250 worth of rubles, (at eight to the dollar) per family. The sum looks heaven-high, at rubles rated 8 to 1 (instead of the legal 4 to 1), and if the calculated prices were those of the peak wide-open market. The intention probably, the effect certainly, is to convey to those being informed an impression of remarkable rural prosperity under collectivization, and attendant peasant satisfactions.

"The Socialized Agriculture of the U.S.S.R.", 837 pages, by the Stanford University Press, 1949, passes in the non-Soviet world as the most authoritative work on the subject. To quote the author, Dr. Naum Jasny: "The official assertion that the expansion of the well-to-do in the village life (of Russia) was greatly promoted by collectivization must be classed with the greatest lies of history."

Since 1938, the Soviets have withheld forthright statistics from the public. That year they published the diminutive figure of 376 rubles as the cash income returned to the average collective household across the Soviet Union. Dr. Jasny's people, on the ground in 1937, found that the households investigated averaged 1806.6 rubles in cash returns. The differing average of some 1400 rubles in the earlier year came, of course, from the sales off the small private plots and those out of the collective deliveries in kind. None of those would be a matter of State record. At 8 to 1 that return amounts to $227.50. The distance between those dollars and the $11,250 bananza, to be bona fide, would have to be made up out of the family's consumption plus an incredible outburst of productivity in an intervening decade—a calculation possibly only by a Munchausen.

Another Author's Approach to Understanding Russia

To discuss Soviet Russia without reference to Dr. Vera Micheles Dean of the Foreign Policy Association would be by-passing one of the ablest experts. Mrs. Dean's "Russia—Menace or Promise" and her "Russia at War and Peace (20 Key Questions and Answers)" (1942) illustrate how the writer cancelled out menacing fear in her own mind and sets out to reassure others. The two publications present much identical material. The first named has the later date of issue.

The author chooses to take the Kremlin trustfully. From the text, it appears unjustly accused of being despotic and of ruling the Russians by methods and with objectives which create an abyss between East and West, thus endangering peace. This is not said directly. The technique is to "let facts speak for themselves." The version given of Communist character and deeds rarely varies from that presented by the Kremlin itself. The position taken and kept throughout is that of one trying to accept affirmative construction of Soviet fundamentals. A reader of the pages who adopts the conclusion they are meant to convey will have erased from his mind much if not all concept of Moscow's "Menace."

Among the methods used, Mrs. Dean applies identical terms to conditions of a different character, terms such as "democracy," "freedom," "rights," "secret police," "imperialism" and so forth. An American reader, having no direct experience of what the terms convey on the Russian side, naturally falls back on what he comprehends by them according to his own experience.

Attempts to normalize the regime put its defects and failures on the same level as those found everywhere else. The effect blurs the sharp demarcations that unfortunately separate East and West. Thus "the Russians think not merely in national but in world terms"—a phrase that turns attention from the major issue whether the Soviet Union constitutes the base for world revolution. The promoters being viewed as "internationalists," can such be so bad after all? Efforts to keep the issues in terms of normal power politics will be noted at large as a practice of this "School," and of other publicists who look upon the Soviet social order with more admiration than objectivity.

The chapter "What was the Bolshevik Revolution?" describes that convulsion as fundamentally agrarian, led by a group of intellectuals (as if vicariously). It completely denatures the "Bolsheviki" and the character of their undertaking—a small minority out (at least so they say themselves) to destroy the existing social structures of mankind. They have gone far on the Russian job, patterned after what they designed for the rest of the world. As far as they have proceeded successfully, incredible brutalities have overtaken those who resist.

The next chapter curiously becomes "Government versus Peasants." Here "following a bad harvest in 1933, the peasants endured a severe famine during the winter of 1933-34 which, according to the estimates of some American correspondents, took a toll of between two and four million lives." (No diplomatic report from Moscow gave a figure lower than 5,000,000). "Some observers believe that the government might have alleviated the hardships of the peasants by releasing grain from its storehouses, but decided not to do so in order to break peasant resistance and speed collectivization." Nothing is said about the utter ruthlessness with which collectivization was carried through, or the deportation and extermination of other millions of people. An example of unpleasant facts minimized, or made to appear improbable ("some observers"). "Hardships" is the word used, when starvation of the millions is what they actually suffered. Soviet health statistics exhibit an excess of 5,500,000 deaths in this period over comparative spaces of time.

When reaching the all-important issue of the State Police, Mrs. Dean finds millions of slave workers in forced labor camps "to some extent explainable." It is not mentioned that the majority are jailed for political reasons, many on mere suspicion. This description of the workings of Soviet justice sounds innocent enough: "In political cases the government exercises judicial powers as well, and persons accused of crimes against the State are seldom brought before ordinary tribunals. The Supreme Court of the Union is first and foremost an organ . . . devoted to the task of protecting the State against hostile elements." Then comes the disarming understatement in the same context: "Lack of separation of powers, however, creates little confusion in practice, since the administrative structure is subordinate to the single control of the Communist Party." This matter, of course, is of the utmost importance, for more is involved in the "separation of powers" than "confusion." The reader should have been told that this fact in itself constitutes a clear, sharp demarcation between totalitarianism and democracy.

This next adventure into the "character" of Soviet Foreign Policy (and there are others) should not be missed: "Russia has lost no opportunity, at gatherings of the United Nations, to indicate its readiness to serve as a spokesman for the people of dependent areas, for the oppressed of the world. This new internationalism on the part of Russia has troubled the United States and Britain, who regard it as a form of interference by Moscow with dependent peoples, especially in the colonies." The subtle turn of this phrase indicates that the author deprecates this attitude on the part of the two "capitalistic" countries. The drop falls on the "Iron Curtain's" existence, the obvious aim to draw the "liberated" countries into the Soviet orbit, the exclusion of any sort of foreign influence from the Soviet domain, the exasperating Moscow propaganda here and in England—all as though our only concern were over dependencies and colonies.

One paragraph on "What is Imperialism" embodies the effort to make the Soviet brand of it justifiable on moral grounds. "What Russia has done during the inter-war years is to make an investment in ideas, instead of capital, in neighboring backward countries." This gives Soviet-Comintern expansion a lofty ethical tone. Mrs. Dean's paragraph "Territory for Self-defense" follows the usual sympathetic line justifying Soviet annexations on that ground. It "does not mean that today Russia is trying to set up governments composed solely of Communists." A statement so patently contrary to common knowledge evokes its own refutation.

Four pages in "Russia at War" with an arresting finale, range discursively over the question whether there is freedom of religion. The nearest to an affirmative that can be located reads: "No active measures of repression were taken against people who went into church to pray." The State attack on religion is then clearly set forth in juxtaposition: ". . . all possible ways of influencing public opinion . . . were employed to make a mockery of religious superstitions and beliefs," which ". . . only the most determined people . . . could withstand." In the educational policy there "was every possibility that, as the older generation passed from the scene, the Soviet Union would have a population entirely brought up in an attitude of indifference or actual contempt for religion."

Explanations for the hostility follow. These appear calculated to cushion the shock of the believing world at a government campaign against all religious movements alike. They take the familiar line pursued by the understanders: "the backwardness of Russia in 1917"; complicity of the official Church through identification of its hierarchy with Tsarist reactionary and repressive measures; "superstitions that had clustered around the ritual." Something probably meant to ease apprehensions, where presumably a government based on Marxist doctrine might come into power, is volunteered "out of Western experiences." "The presence in the state of liberal and social-minded churchmen tends to reduce social and economic frictions, and thus to diminish the danger of violent revolt against organized religion." The head of the Society of the Militant Godless left the Sherwood Eddy Seminar group in Moscow in 1932 under no such impression with this biting testimony:

"Our militant atheism is absolutely related to our revolutionary world view. It is a basic constituent. It is not a sort of appendage, which has developed only under conditions of the Soviet Union . . . Therefore we struggled energetically against all religion and in this case made no difference between a 'good' religion and a 'bad' one. On the contrary, we declared that the finer types of religion demanded an even more acute struggle. Lenin declared that the difference between a 'good' and a 'bad' religion was the same as between a blue and a violet devil."

Emil Yaroslavsky, the speaker, had not discerned with Mrs. Dean that "Communism, when unadulterated by political considerations, prescribes a way of life similar to that which is urged by the most highly developed religious movements. Communism has as its avowed objective the improvement of living conditions for the 'oppressed toiler.' This ideal is not so far removed as it sometimes seems from the ideals of early Christianity. . . . In the practice of Communism, as in the practice of Christianity, however, there is often a great gap between aspiration and achievement." Which leaves the two something like parallel beneficent forces for mankind's good in Mrs. Dean's view.

An imperishable witness of Russian bishops (of the Church left unrelievedly reactionary by Mrs. Dean) runs to the contrary, and belongs here in the record. In 1926, some forty of them in exile on the Arctic island of Solovki petitioned the Soviet Government to stand aloof from the religions question. The bishops first made clear that the points of discord did not lie at all in the accepted matters of state concern. The Church stood aside from the new repartition of wealth, the nationalization of property and the organization of political authority. In all Church history these have been recognized as domains of the state. The discord arose from the irreconcilability of the spiritual teachings of the Church with the materialism of the Communist party and the state's enforcement of that philosophy upon the national mind. Then followed their solemnizing and imperishable witness in these words.

"The Church recognizes the spiritual principle: communism denies it. The Church believes in the living God, Creator of the world, Giver of its life and fate: communism does not admit His existence; believes that the world was self organized, and that no reasonable principles or purposes govern its history. The Church believes in the steadfast principles of morality, justice and law: communism looks upon them as the conditional results of class struggle, and values moral questions only from the standpoint of their usefulness. The Church instills the feeling of that humility which elevates man's soul: communism abases man through his pride. For the Church religion is not only the living force enabling man to attain his heavenly destiny, but also the source of all that is greatest in human relations; which is the foundation of earthly welfare, happiness and the health of nations. For communism religion is the opium that drugs the nations, that weakens their energy, that is the source of their poverty and misfortunes. With such deep differences in fundamental principles, . . . it becomes impossible that an inner nearness or reconciliation could exist between them. There can be no reconciliation between assertion and negation, between yes and no."

Thus skills, however adroit, employed to make the Soviet Power appear in the role of the misunderstood, even persecuted benefactor of the underprivileged, liberator of the oppressed, break down in the face of its own words and deeds. Official party statements of supreme objectives are never found reading that way for the inner circles. The eleven top Communists of America were not sentenced for teaching in felicitous phrases the marching orders of communism to the students they were training to become party cadres. Neither in China nor on any other advance front do the Red leaders, trained to type from Moscow and held to performance by its agents on the ground, agitate, print or broadcast in the pacific language of the "School for Understanding." When Chinese Mao gave the world his reasons for tying to Soviet Russia as against orientation with the West, his statement read as though he had before him this paragraph out of the Program of the Third International adopted in Moscow in 1928—authentic marching terms never renounced by any spokesman for the Comintern, Russian party, or Soviet government. It is now in open worldwide operation and effect:

> "The Class struggle, which hitherto was conducted in circumstances when the proletariat was not in possession of State power, is now being conducted on an enormous and really world scale. The working class of the world has now its own state—the one and only fatherland of the international proletariat. . . . The world coalition of capital, unstable, internally corroded, but armed to the teeth, is confronted by a single world coalition of Labor. Thus as a result of the first round of imperialist wars, a new, fundamental antagonism has arisen of world historical scope and significance; the antagonism between the U.S.S.R. and the capitalist world."

Some Discern Strictly, or Chiefly, Power Politics

Another view of the Russian scene, disassociated quite from that of the "Understanders" school, can be had from the position of a one hundred per cent believer in power politics. A book "In Defense of the National Interest"* sets forth and expounds lucidly the thesis that the Kremlin plans and operates on the power level purely, and so can be successfully and safely dealt with on that ground alone. One sees the shade and doctrine of Nietzsche in the background. And most of the civilized world has moved rather far in aspirations, efforts and hopes from that dark and bloody ground in the wide field of international relations. The other view, nevertheless, is shared here in brief with our readers, as a position not altogether ruled out. One power aspect appears, and is treated at length, in our later pages. Yet vigorous dissent has to be taken with the proposition that power ambition alone, or chiefly, accounts for Kremlin motivation and strategy. Dissent also with the implication that fundamental moralities may properly be sacrificed to the national interest.

The author of "In Defense of the National Interest," now to be cited, is Professor Hans J. Morgenthau, Director of the University of Chicago Center for the Study of American Foreign Policy. He spends no time on the

---

* Knopf, New York, 1951.

vices or virtues of communism, nor on Soviet revolutionary ideology and strategy as such, beyond the generalization that a head on conflict exists "between two kinds of moral principles, two types of moral conduct, two ways of life." The East-West embroilment, as he presents it, reduces to the single issue of "Russian imperialism, and Communist revolution only in so far as it is an instrument of that imperialism." And by way of emphasis: "This is not a struggle between good and evil, truth and falsehood, but of power with power."

From here the hard-boiled power politics advocate takes over. He elevates national interest to "moral dignity." On this height success seems to justify, or at least to warrant, over-riding other moral grandeurs, since "all the successful statesmen of modern times from Richelieu to Churchill have made the national interest the ultimate standard of their policies, and none of the great moralists in international affairs has attained his goals." Great powers traditionally keep agreements, it is confessed, only so long as they serve the national interest. Cited are the example of "Perfidious Albion," Cavour, and the Germans reducing their guarantee of Belgian neutrality to "a scrap of paper" in July of 1914. The forty violations (Author's count) of international agreements by the Russians we face "differ only in matter and form." It follows that more dishonoring can be anticipated until agreements covering the map can be arrived at that accord with the Soviet Union interest.

Over against the Soviet practice of stern realism, the Professor indicts American foreign policy and prevailing American thinking for "Utopianism," and proceeds with samples of our dreaming of "a political world that never existed," of fancying power politics would be banished by a United Nations, and that the purpose of fighting is "consummated with victory and the downfall of the aggressor."

Franklin Roosevelt at Teheran had not learned the lesson taught by the fate of "Wilsonianism." Humanitarian ideals as expressed in the Atlantic Charter and the Four Freedoms governed the President's course, "unrelated to the concrete distribution of power which the United States had a vital interest in creating and maintaining after the end of hostilities." America insured a Russia as now faced on the continent, it is argued, by being party to the over-all Allied strategy which, on the defeat of Germany, eventuated in establishing the Red Armies in power over Eastern and Southeast Europe. The Yalta stipulations concerning free elections and democratic governments "were a mere illusion if they were supposed to have any reference to the sharing of control over the countries concerned." The course of insistence on their observance, is characterized as barren legalism.

Dr. Morgenthau lays out yet stronger prescriptions for curing the chronic ills of our foreign policy, currently and presumably for all time. Under the taboo of "Sentimentalism" he rejects, as ultimates of policy objectives and motivations, such moral principles and values as "gratitude, common dedi-

cation to liberty, manifest destiny, . . . support of democracy, good neigh-
borliness, generosity." Political actions so inspired have been "bent to
conform to moral abstractions, political requirements have been subordinated
to moral ones, and in the process political success has been sacrificed without
appreciable gain in universal morality." Trading in spheres of influence
receives sanction under this lofty "moral dignity" of national interest. And,
if it calls for the sacrifice of another power or of lesser peoples, that goes
into the price of success as well.

This all seems to add up to the national necessity and righteousness of
these United States, innerly toughened and outwardly armored, confronting
the masters of the other Super-Power on purely power terms—their own
—inasmuch as these alone rule the world of political reality. Not only
so, the Doctor bluntly poses the alternative of give and take "Negotiation" in this spirit, or of "War." The Soviet Union, he reports, has
made numerous proposals (never officially acknowledged by Washington)
"for the division of the world into two gigantic spheres of influence, one
dominated by the Soviet Union with Western influence excluded, the other
free from Soviet domination and under the influence of the United States."

Arnold Toynbee is quoted as suggesting in a Columbia University lecture
in 1948 "a provisional partition of the world into a Russian and an American
sphere by agreements between the two." The great historian thought it
would give us time, among other things, "to try gradually to build these two
spheres together and eventually to unite them in a cooperative world government." And Churchill too would still give all out bargaining a try probably.
The author calls him up as something like a character witness out of the
January 23, 1948, speech in the House of Commons, when Churchill advised
that the Western democracies "at the earliest possible moment, take the
initiative in asking the Soviet for a settlement," and added:

"It is idle to reason or argue with the Communists. It is, however, possible
to deal with them on a fair, realistic basis, and, in my experience, they will
keep their bargains as long as it is in their interest to do so, which might
in this grave matter be a long time, once things were settled."

The Professor elsewhere has safeguarded the flanks and rear of his
"power" position with this reservation: "If the Soviet Union pursues the
goal of world revolution, it can attain that goal only by conquering the Western world first and making it communistic afterwards."

World Revolutionary Purpose Discounted

We bring another writer into the forum with an outlook entitled to attention because materials lie around the place sufficiently to lend some plausi-
bility to an aphorism that the Soviet Union system is essentially "a Russian
response to a Russian situation." Edward Crankshaw in "Cracks in the

Kremlin Wall"* labors assiduously to present this Russia as essentially Russian politically, with the force of onetime world revolutionary communism in wraps, if not outmoded.

The author knows a lot about Russians, particularly on the human side, and likes the masses of good ones. During the last war he served with a British Mission in the country for a period and returned there in 1947 in a visitor's capacity. To set all witchhunters at ease, let this passage reflect his view of the men centrally directing the Soviet system: "the only group of people in the world today which is actively and deliberately, and for whatever reason, committed to the downfall of our society." Without arguing down in detail the main position he takes, the totality of the text of "The Russia We Face Now," we think, renders it untenable.

The Crankshaw thesis runs on thiswise:

1. Lenin transferred from the domestic to the international scene the class war teaching of Karl Marx, who saw the world revolutionary upheaval proceeding country by country indigenously on the whole, each having to produce its own revolution, to occur at a particular point in its economic-social development and in its own way. Lenin though made the Soviet Union "the first base of the world revolution," invoking a conflict between two world systems that would eventuate in the downfall and extinction of one or the other. He saw world revolution achieved only "through a series of bloody conflicts between nations." Peaceful coexistence could be "no more than temporary." The author attaches to the resulting brand of socialism the term that Lenin and his partisans proudly applied and used— "Bolshevism." The Comintern became its international implement, "a monopoly of the Bolsheviks."

2. Stalin "has taken Marxism out of Leninism," a development that grew from the necessity of erecting and defending the base before world revolution could be projected from it successfully. The interests of world revolution and of the Soviet state came into conflict, resolved progressively in the period by the Comintern becoming an instrument of Soviet foreign policy. "Socialism in one country" became the slogan. The effects are represented to have translated the proletarian revolution into the Russian industrial revolution, exalted Russian nationalism internally, and, beyond that, constrained world communism into the channels of Great Russian imperialism. "So that today we are faced no longer with a hostile group of Bolsheviks who happen to be Russians, but by a hostile group of Russians who happen to be Bolsheviks, and who have more or less fashioned the government of a great power in their own image."

3. Stalinists, we are told, fight in what they conceive to be the interests of the Soviet Union rather than of revolutionary socialism. Although with

The Viking Press, 1952.

64

Moscow's insistence communism and Russian have become identified, they have "no intrinsic connection with each other." The Generalissimo receives absolution from any world revolutionary purpose or planned program of the sort. This position so counters prevailing beliefs that a trio out of several repetitious assertions of it will be put down here. To get to grips with what Stalin "really does believe" and to "form an image of the Soviet reality," approach "with a clear head" is possible "only if we abandon the idea of a grand Bolshevik design, patiently and deliberately worked out over a period of thirty years." In fact, all the evidence we have points to the conclusion that, far from having a considered plan of attack, Stalin, from Teheran onwards, has been improvising in a hand-to-mouth manner . . ." "There is nothing at all to suggest that in 1945 Stalin saw the formal sovietization of Poland, Czechoslovakia, Hungary, and the rest as a goal to be worked for in a hurry."

Still the ghost of Marx haunts the premises. Through Kremlin wall cracks, Stalin gets glimpsed "enough of a Marxist . . . to be obsessed with the disintegrating tendencies of the modern capitalistic society . . ." His Marxism is said to contain two principles (most important ones we think); "the general proposition of the advancing proletarian revolution, and the particular proposition of the manner of its advance." It is explained that Stalin recognizes them as already "gone aground." . . . "But by the bulk of the Moscow Communists they are not abandoned." As an aside, the point must here be pressed for all to see, that both propositions are employed worldwide by the Cominform as vigorously as the Comintern ever did, and now with full open Soviet Union backing. The bugles that were blown in the three orations at Stalin's bier sounded nothing like "retreat." Accordingly, large import needs to be read into another of the quoted author's passages (which he seems most of the time to seek to invalidate). It is to the effect that the "whole outlook" of Stalin himself was "colored and, indeed heavily conditioned by Marxist modes of thought."

Tito's challenge, Crankshaw thinks, "forced the Kremlin's hand. And this is important. It brings us around to our beginning, which was to disassociate Russia and communism. Russia is Russia, an unsettling influence in the world, timeless, a formidable force . . . and certainly, as Russia, not concerned with the conquest of the world but only with assuring her own dominant position. Communism as a revolutionary movement is also formidable . . . Russia and communism taken separately can neither of them conquer the world. But Russia and communism taken together form a combination terrible indeed"—an "extraordinary accident of association" between external Russia and a misguided genuine movement to improve the human lot. The connection provides the ruling class in Russia "with a body of hocus-pocus which offers the answer to every question as well as a sense of continuity, and outside harnesses the energies of Communists everywhere to the Kremlin's egocentric purpose."

The later pages could ease up Western nerves, if the data offered be wholly accepted. ". . . the whole training of the Communist party is against any sort of aggressive war that cannot be finished quickly, . . . reinforced by the traditional Russian reluctance to storm a strong position if it can be undermined. Add to that the almost certain fact that the Soviet Union . . . is in no fit state to risk embroiling herself in a total war, either materially or morally." Material resources there for carrying on long all-out war compared with the West are made to appear hopelessly disparate. Just the cold war basis presses the people beyond further burdening. The "Peace" policy has the design in part to solace them and influence loyalty to their protector from war. No observer in Moscow in autumn, 1941, "could believe for one moment that the Soviet Union could hold together under American bombing." The Soviet economy for years to come is rated incapable of "standing the strain of total mobilization." But as insurance: "This does not mean we should not be prepared for attack."

AN IMPASSE ABSOLUTE?

Effort has been made thus far to present a rounded, however concise, picture of such solid facts as condition today's Russia vis-a-vis the United States, the West and the World. The data presented have sketched the national history, the basic human and physical resources, the principles of Communist rule and its over-all program, the functioning of the subservient Soviet government, its people's predicament, and certain international reactions.

In this section we cover less tangible but possibly more important ground, the whys and wherefores in the moves of the Russian leadership. We seek thereby to ascertain whether we are confronted with an impasse absolute, or if there is any chance of making effective contact with them in mutuality of interest.

Proceeding by Deduction

The military man has long told us that to know the enemy's plans means the battle is half won. While in the political-economic field any set of conclusions drawn from the available facts on Soviet Russia's plans involves guesswork, yet the necessity remains to proceed and with as careful guessing as can be done.

One fact is clear, the Communist leaders are arch realists. But the companion truth is equally clear to those who have studied their conduct closely. They are also theorists to a degree seldom met among statesmen. They conduct their daily affairs ruled by a philosophical system which is described as Marxist-Leninist-Stalinist. Major moves are made according to their interpretation of that system. It is this duality that must be kept in mind in searching for the clues to their plans and methods.

Karl Marx in Soviet Diplomacy

With the highlighting of power politics to the near exclusion of other motivations, the assumption is often made that the Soviet leaders deal only in such terms. This oversimplification has led many an observer astray.

Stalin brought Karl Marx into modern diplomacy via the "adjustment" of the Simon-pure doctrine to the present situation. Malenkov's funeral oration credited "the great thinker of our age" with having "creatively developed in new historic conditions the teachings of Marxism and Leninism."

The Marxian doctrine of the incompatibility between the capitalist and Communist orders of society has been used as the times suited, most conspicuously during the years immediately following the military alliance in World War II.

Another dogma is contained in the Marxian prediction that capitalist countries will weaken each other by "imperialist wars." This doubtless activated Stalin in some measure in signing the 1939 pact with Hitler. The great war that was unleashed would be calculated to allow Russia to become the real beneficiary of the struggle between the capitalist nations.

A third feature of Marxism that has application in Soviet diplomacy today is the doctrine of harassing capitalism in its colonial and half-colonial possessions so long as direct attack is deemed unpropitious. On this ground the Kremlin fomented revolution in China in 1925. Much later, the same pattern showed itself in harrying the United States on the far distant Korean mainland. For in the Soviet view, the United States is an empire and its imperial influence, if not its rule, extends all the way to Korea.

A fourth Marxist theory applicable to modern Soviet diplomacy is that depressions must inevitably ensue to weaken and eventually destroy capitalist societies. When Professor Varga erstwhile economic authority of Moscow, was unable to forecast with assurance the great depression that must befall the United States at the close of the last war, he lost permanent favor at the Kremlin. For Marx had long since declared that this must happen to a capitalist nation upon the conclusion of a major war.

A value of Marxist teachings to Soviet leaders is found in the "consistency" it gives their conduct. Being at the same time rationalists, they must deal on a day-by-day basis with their problems. Yet to some degree such conduct lacks order, which is supplied by their overriding Marxist theories. Probably of equal importance, Marxian theories and prophecies fire the imagination of Communists and impart to their plans an integration and drive that seems lacking in Washington statecraft.

Yet the reader must be reminded of the other quality that rules Kremlin conduct, namely, its realism. Here power politics takes over. It forces Soviet leaders to unusual lengths, such as breaking agreements with erstwhile allies without any regard to honor in order to secure Russia's sensitive borders by the forceful creation of buffer satellite states.

Some Reasonable Conjectures as to Their Strategy

The Kremlin strategy in world affairs is complex, made so in no small measure by desire to keep us guessing as to Soviet plans and program. We have given them every needed evidence of our concerns and fears. They know how avidly we search every rumor, test every passing wind for the answers to such disturbing questions as—Does the post-Stalin group really want peace? Or, are they making peace gestures to mislead us into letting down our guard of which they may take quick advantage? Or, are they aware of stresses inside Russia and need peace to cement their structure of control? Or, are they capitalizing on this desire of ours for peace, during which they will major on fomenting revolution in situations ripe for it? Or, have they reached the judgment that a period of relative peace will aid their cause by weakening if not destroying NATO and other European alliances?

The Kremlin planners know that a highly industrialized society like ours, with seventy per cent of our people resident in compact cities, is exceedingly vulnerable to attack, and that our people are aware of this. They know the value of preying on anxiety and fear. They think they stand to gain from the corroding effects of the Damocles sword which they hold suspended over our heads. Their invention of the cold war in permanence serves that purpose.

Despite what they learned of the fighting quality of American soldiers, they have noted our mechanical civilization and labor under an impression that misled Hitler. For the Soviet leaders believe us to be too soft to withstand sudden, wholesale disaster rained down on us from the sky. They believe the resulting chaos would be prostrating here. By comparison, the Russians would fare much better, being closer to the earth. "A pancake cannot topple over."

They have deep concern over our determined defense buildup. Yet they calculate even this to be no total gain for us, as it drains off our economic strength into unproductive outlets. The tensions and disunity which this entails is their gain. Their own armament program is not felt by the populace in the same way. Its cost is entirely concealed in the Soviet system of major financing by extractions from the social product at its source more than through direct taxation. Sacrifice there is reflected only in the continuance of low living standards of the people, to which long years of attrition have inured them.

With these considerations in mind, the Kremlin leaders have pursued a cold war policy with apparent confidence. Their expectation of its effect on us is based on such reasoning as the foregoing. Behind it lies the Marxist assumption that such pressure continued long enough would yield them total victory through the collapse of capitalism by war or by other means.

Soviet Nonchalance in Grave Circumstances

In the cold war, or any hot war which might follow, the Communist leaders put their faith in their understanding of and control over the "masses." They note with relish the way Western diplomats look askance at this Marxian term. They are aware of the finality embodied in an atomic war. While they may not be anxious to risk it, nothing would prevent them doing so if it proves inescapable in the march on the way to the final victory of communism. In which event they believe they will be ultimate possessors of the field, their remnant the only group able to organize the survivors, and their social pattern the only one applicable in the chaos.

69

Whether with Guns or by Strangulation

Being who and what they are, Communists hold the ultimate elimination of the capitalist social order to be inevitable. This may come about either by war or by internal collapse through revolution. In the systematic Kremlin mind the two are linked together to form a single design of attack-strategy.

In this view, a peace program creates one of the interludes that lulls the opponent until the "historic moment" arrives for the revolutionary pushover as economic instability grows to unmanageable proportions. Or, advantage may be taken of an exposed position such as existed in South Korea after the evacuation of American forces to seize and hold territory by direct military action. Or, again, peace may be strained almost to the breaking point, only to be relieved from pressure by an abrupt about-face, as they did after forcing on us the airlift to feed Berlin in the vain attempt to drive us from that city.

Nor need we expect the end of this attack-strategy is at hand. Whether it takes the form of a peace approach or otherwise, it is to be remembered that such maneuvers are planned features in the Kremlin program.

Moscow Outguessed Washington

When the war ended, Russia faced only one other great military power, the United States. But this country was not intent upon remaining an armed camp. It sought instead to put into practice a belief in "One World." The ruling Communists, on the other hand, have always regarded Russia in one light as a means of achieving the world revolution. To that extent, the land, the people and their resources are expendable.

However grave the circumstances, Communist policies dealing with them emanate from a single center, tailored to the central pattern of the unshakeable will. To pass over the multiple of Allies to coordinate policy, the American government as a Democracy has to cope ceaselessly with divergent wills among its people in order to establish a prevailing public opinion supporting its position. No such time consuming and frustrating experience confronts the Soviet dictatorship. With authority and policy centering in one room, the Red leaders may and do change fronts and alter strategy regardless of Russian public opinion. They make and remake that opinion or ignore it at will. This gives the Vishinskys, once they get their orders, a professional nonchalance removed from the harassments that beset the Western diplomat.

Finally, the ever-present dread of all-out war casting gloom over all free nations conditions action in Western chancelleries. While this must give pause to the Kremlin leaders, it is not outside their customary and current calculations. They recognize war as a wholly orthodox, legitimate means of destroying capitalism within a country, and freely employable to the same end in international situations. This imparts to the Kremlin leaders a certain professional detachment and approach not allowed to their opposite numbers in the West.

From the Kremlin's viewpoint, American concern for peace, and for the establishment of a United Nations organization to promote it, was motivated largely by desire to preserve the status quo in the aftermath of war's confusion. The course chosen there has been to avoid head-on collision with a militarily strong America and still to make the most of the rich "pickings" that the war had left lying around. This was vigorously done. The first order of business obtained control over that belt of nations on Russia's European borders where the presence of Soviet armies would insure nonresistance. As America disbanded her armies, and reaffirmed allegiance to earlier Wilsonian principles of international conduct, Poland, Czechoslovakia, Rumania and Bulgaria fell. Greece escaped by a hair's breadth. Tito mutinied rather than become an enslaved puppet of Moscow. The German East Zone was rapidly converted into a Soviet colony.

These were events that in any former era of dominant power politics would have resulted in a major war between leading powers. And the failure of the United States to react in this traditional manner to such provocation may have caused wonderment inside the Kremlin, as it evidently did. For they could not believe that we had discarded the usual territorial gains concept of victory for one which sought peaceful international settlement of disputes based on national integrity. They probably judged us weak.

On our part we did not adjust quickly to such Soviet conduct. It took repeated examples of aggression culminating in the effort to destroy freedom in Greece to throw America into reverse.

The prices that the free world paid for our failure to anticipate and to thwart Soviet postwar aggressive purposes cannot be calculated. They have not yet all been paid. But dear as the lesson has come, if well learned by now, as we face what appears to be widescale Kremlin overtures for a peace period, there remains time to defeat them.

Why Not War Already?

In the period following relinquishment of our World War II military might, and even as late as 1951, experts agree that the Red armies could have overrun Europe almost at will. Yet the attempt was not made. Why, if a tactic of Bolshevik communism is the use of force to destroy existing capitalist states, was it not employed in such an advantageous situation?

The experts of one school believe that the Kremlin responds to the "long view." This holds that without any risk of power or impairment of resources communism will inherit the lands and peoples of capitalist nations after their economic collapse from the internal disorders which that system suffers and is unable to cure. That the European countries are helpless and far advanced

71

towards the disintegrating stages of economic and political disease. In this view, in a period of "peace" the disorders will advance and in due time the victims will fall easily to limited, or even bloodless, force.

Experts of another school see in the continuing cold war and the periodic hot flashes of fighting (as in Korea) a belligerent Soviet diplomacy that better accounts for Kremlin conduct since 1945. Not willing to risk a premature showdown in a European conflict, the effort has been to continue the pressure of uncertainty and doubt through unfriendly, often bitter cold war diplomacy and warlike postures, highly provocative and always carrying the threat of contemplated war. This transpired with monotonous regularity at the United Nations and elsewhere over the world. With the Western powers having offered a peaceful world at Yalta and Potsdam and Stalin apparently acceding, any explanation falls short that does not indicate this Soviet belligerency as being a willingness to risk ultimate conflict.

Today's more peaceful gestures can be safely considered as fitting into another strategy of the "intervals," a maneuver whereby a longer or shorter period of time can be employed to cultivate a degree of more normal social intercourse between Communist and capitalist nations. Examination of Kremlin policy since 1917 reveals a number of such intervals. But it also shows the consistency of purpose on the part of the Kremlin to force the eventual downfall of capitalist nations in destruction either helped on by revolution or through revolution helped on by war.

On Soviet Overconfidence

History has always had a way of bypassing grand plans and total strategies. One would wish the new leaders in the Kremlin were better students of it. It would be helpful, too, if their intelligence were higher concerning the state of affairs in the United States and among the free world nations. Contrary to the hopes of the Communists, time is not running out on a tired "Old West." While the cold war has exerted much strain on the people and the resources of the free world, it has not exhausted powers of great resistance. On the contrary, there has been brought into being such solidarity of international purpose and effort as never before witnessed in peacetime.

A gigantic flanking movement is under way that bids fair to envelop the entire Communist position. This began with the early successes of the Marshall Plan in preventing the collapse and starting the economic recovery of war stricken nations; moved on to the establishment of NATO, the Organization for European Economic Cooperation, and Point Four with its large promise for the underdeveloped areas where tension is rife; the UN health, agricultural, welfare and educational organizations in which the Soviet Union refuses to participate; and such outstanding achievements as the Schuman Plan. Much remains to be done, but this beginning ought to give the new Kremlin responsibles pause as they flex their muscles and before becoming too confident about revolutionary success. Could it be that all this has finally come home to them? Could such knowledge deflect them from their belligerent course to once again seek ameliorative roads to negotiation?

Bolshevist Suspiciousness

John Fischer has called the Kremlin leaders "men of fear." Distrust has played no small part in moulding their individual characters and shaping their conduct. This is a major fact to be confronted.

Any Communist leader who emerges on the world stage has been subjected since childhood to training that has sacrificed to a "cause" his individual morality. He is animated by an overriding ideal, a complete purpose, the "liberation of the world proletariat," the "worldwide victory of communism." He is as much an indoctrinated soul as was any authentic German Nazi in the infallibility of Hitler. His discipline and actions serve the cause unswervingly, without question.

The arrogance displayed by Communist leaders in their dealings with Western diplomats is in no small part a cover up for the inner insecurity they feel. They cannot have intercourse in any normal way with representatives from the capitalist nations they have been taught to despise without assuming an attitude of superior infallibility that they do not really feel. This is especially true of those who learn at first hand the facts of life beyond the borders of Russia, the amazing contrast between what they had been taught and what really exists.

Communist suspiciousness has an official origin, being a residue of the Marxist doctrine of incompatibility. It has been institutionalized in Russia, forming no small part of the secret police and spy system imposed on all from the highest official to the lowliest worker. It is so infectious as to develop nationwide distrust and fear.

Such a deep-seated characteristic does not lend itself readily to change. It thrusts a stumbling block in the way of meeting the Russian leaders on common ground. It remains long after good relationships have been formed between normal peoples and nations.

On Coexistence

The Western mind often turns to the prospect of existing in one peaceful world with the Communist nations. We assume that some "comrades," too, dwell on such a prospect. Malenkov has repeated Stalin's observations that such a happy state can be achieved. But the Generalissimo's pronouncements uniformly had conditioning context, and they never offered safeguards against the possibility of their one-sided nullification by Moscow without warning and with all the old evil consequences. Poles like Mikolajchek and Czechs like Benes entered into coexistence relationships in good faith but with disastrous results for their people.

Yet a pause that would allow for peaceful coexistence could present advantages to the West. Time builds in our favor, both in furthering military strength for defense against any lurking aggression; and in the strengthening of those economic forces in the free world for stabilizing the economy against any shock.

For the Kremlin a period of peaceful coexistence would prove most beneficial in the initial stages of the transfer of power to the succession. The moves in so many different quarters so soon after taking over suggests they had been planned this way in advance of the demise. The wise Stalin was capable of as much.

Beyond this immediate time, much depends on what internal forces play upon the conduct of the new leadership. In the rapid growth of Soviet Russia a new industrial revolution has taken place. From it Russia is emerging the second industrial power in the world. The very structure of this new machine economy requires many of the practices of any industrial society. The cultural revolution that accompanies it can have far-reaching effects. Some of these could materially ameliorate Soviet policy, or even change its destiny.

For example, Paul Wohl in the New York Herald Tribune of March 27, 1953, writes of the "Red technocrats" thrusting up as engineers and managers —20,000,000 of them who "live with and by the party state. They are the men with whom the new middle class identifies itself . . . engineers, foremen, technicians and 'shock workers,' the 'lower commanders of industry.' . . . They are the pride of the party, the props of the state."

As for the satellite peoples, in a time less tense we expect to see them free again. In a period of peaceful coexistence, opportunity may be present to establish such relationships with other nations as will ameliorate their plight and bring nearer the day of their freedom. It is even remotely possible that such a period could see China making overtures on her own towards the West.

Thus, "iffys" aside, coexistence achieved with full safeguards against surprise attacks could prove beneficial to the wide world. The absence of war itself must be counted a gain. Over against this summary respecting coexistence, must be placed the record of unsatisfactory experience with the Kremlin ever since the Lenin seizure of power in 1917. Pending establishment of a peaceful, workable *system* of coexistence, it would seem to promise more to try cushioning the corners of conflict between the free world and Communist Russia.

Searching the Corners

Experience should have taught us the unwisdom of presuming on an overall cushioning process, such as to suddenly dismantle the defense now being achieved, or even to suspend its building up, in order to demonstrate to the Kremlin our pacific purposes. We recall, however, that when confronted with a specific issue, such as making common cause against Hitler, it was possible to achieve relations with the Soviet government that admitted of very large joint efforts and results. This is how the cushioning process must go forward—jointly on a give and take basis—if it is to succeed.

Stalin's peace feelers extended to Hitler during the war, behind the backs of his Allies, show how far he would go in order to achieve a great specific end. Kleist, a minor German official, had been used to transmit such an offer to Ribbentrop in the summer of 1943, and again in 1944. It can be added here that similar advances were made by the Kremlin as early as the last months of 1942. And the Japanese government made parallel efforts up to September 4, 1944, through General Oshima, its Ambassador.

Kleist has recorded, in his "Between Hitler and Stalin," the conversation in which Stalin's middleman, Claus, discussed cautiously but clearly Stalin's reasons. Even if such documentary proof did not exist, Stalin's motive would be obvious. He approached Hitler because he deemed it unbearable for Russia that Germany, Europe's "heartland," should be lost as a buffer against the Western powers whom he considered would become acutely dangerous when America appeared with them at the Russian frontier after the defeat of Germany.

There is no evidence to indicate any change in the Kremlin mind concerning the threat the United States presents in being in Europe directly up against the border of Soviet power. And the Kremlin is still committed to the concept of power politics as the guide in foreign affairs, while the United States is bent upon leading the free world away from adherence to that concept. The prospect of penetrating the Kremlin wall of suspicion and fear is in direct proportion to our ability to convince the Soviet leadership of the sincerity of our pronouncements that we want no territory, and will not engage in any war except as a defensive measure; that our NATO interests are wholly defensive.

The ways in which the East and West conduct their international affairs contrast so widely that the peace of the world may depend finally on whether America can persuade the Russian rulers of the sincerity of her pacific professions. This will not be easy. However, one of the first public addresses of the Secretary of State, John Foster Dulles, contained these courageous lines: "Difficulties have emerged which, at first, were overlooked. But we need not be discouraged. What has to be, can be. When it is suicidal not to have world order, then world order is possible."

Let no mistake be made about the difficulties ahead. There is no panacea, no easy way of shaking off the kind and measure of suspicion held by the Kremlin, no immediate assurance forthcoming from that side that will satisfy all our own just fears and qualms.

Timeliness in Mutual Approaches

Competent reporters say the real reason for Churchill's preinaugural visit to the President-elect was to share his views about the desirability of an early meeting with Stalin. One can assume that such a proposal was not motivated by any last-ditch despairing state of mind. More likely the seasoned British statesman expressed the belief that we are near a point in time when we would hold a strong bargaining hand in this fateful international game of diplomacy.

The free world is better able to defend itself now than at any time since demobilization after World War II. Our military defense rapidly approaches completion of the buildup period. The American public knows better the Russia we face and the necessity of maintaining adequate defenses. It cannot be that all this has escaped Moscow's attention, that the Kremlin leaders are still unaware of the great strength, firmness and staying powers of their opposition. With all this in mind, the passing of Stalin may have given negotiations of both small and large issues improved prospects. But their ultimate success, which means the establishment of peace without debilitating appeasement for some appreciable span of time to come, will depend in considerable degree on how well we understand the fundamental guiding purposes of the Kremlin's new top leadership.

All the evidence is not in as yet, but more than a glimmer of its thinking is before us, enabling some guess-estimates to be made of what the future holds in store there. We see the monolithic power of the party continuing to be applied to its Marxist purposes in its varied alternative or complementary ways. We see clearly the strategy of the "intervals" displayed, the timing of its application depending on the needs of the moment.

Malenkov and company have promptings in their initial forms of internal considerations as well. As with numerous other successions to Russian power in the past, the "amnesty" approach, and easing of the economic yoke offer quieting sedatives to the population. Together with the pacific approach that becomes the motif of current Soviet diplomacy, tensions get eased all around and give the "breather" they seem to need.

The new Kremlin leadership must go on facing two ways at once, looking inward on the problems developing within its borders, and outward at a world which their communism divided into two armed camps.

The hammer and sickle emblem of the Communist Soviet Republic betokens peaceful work. It turns out that a mighty spear, its shaft capped by steel, would better symbolize the real purpose to which this Russia has been dedicated until now. The thrust since 1947 has been aimed aggressively against the free West, and primarily at the heart of America.

A new administration in Washington, nevertheless, without responsibility in past negotiations, is in a certain unprejudiced position for a fresh approach toward findng pacific meeting ground. It is further favored by having at hand the lessons of the past and the now established facts (such as these pages set forth) concerning the nature of Soviet purposes and plans. The pitfalls are well demarked. There would be monstrous folly in indulging any easy assumption that the Kremlin has abandoned the fundamental purpose to effect a Communist world. It would be equally unrealistic to expect a disposition there to enter an effective disarmament program with inspection and control powers adequate to the world's peace. Dangerously absurd therefore to enter any conference with a notion of abandoning the NATO defense effort in order to allay Russia's fears of our military presence on her European border. But workable initiatives do not have to be premised on such "ultimates."

America Faces Herself

We live in a new world, so immensely changed by hyperdimensioned war prospect that the imperative necessity of securing peace compels us to face total solutions as well. Peace is no longer something we entertain as an appealing ideal of doubtful practicality. The stark fact is that the transmutation of this peace ideal into reality is decisive for our survival.

That is why we reluctantly changed plans after the dismantling of our armies at the close of the last world war. The Communist threat became too real to be ignored any longer. We did not abandon for a moment our conviction concerning peace. But we did learn that only by becoming so formidable a fighting force that the Kremlin could not hope to gain its ends by arms, was there any prospect of putting our peaceful intentions to work in the world. "Dealing from strength" appeared the only way to get on with Moscow.

But this preoccupation with growing militarily strong and remaining strong does not set the limits of sound foreign policy. The foremost interest of an America sincere in its peace professions, is to point the way for a Russian state that still operates on the level of XIXth century power politics, to the higher one Western civilization craves to reach—collective security under international law.

The herculean task of such induction may not be shirked, America holds the initiative. Keeping her defense effort strictly of that character and purpose, and moving on aggressively with pronouncements and measures for peace that are realistic and timely, she can take the central position on ethical grounds that must carry increasing weight in the international thought and action of most of mankind. The United States cannot creditably do otherwise than continue to offer leadership toward eventually establishing viable relationships with this Russia, without which no world peace will be possible. The road ahead is not clear, nor is it smooth, but it is the only road along which our nation can go forward to its destiny. Thus armed might and realistic diplomacy hold the immediate priorities if the nation and our institutions are to be preserved in and throughout the present danger.

AFTER ARMS AND POSITIVE DIPLOMACY

It is not the province of this book to go at length beyond the Russia we face here and now, and the critical day and hour demands in national policy. Courses of action to permanently win and maintain security, freedom and the good life for all remain to be pursued with diligence and skill. The longer years are upon us, too, with duties to correspond. Dynamic communism makes its far-flung bid for the minds and wills of persons and of peoples. It is the most challenging social-cultural fact in contemporary life. We shall content ourselves with four pointers to areas of long-time action prescribed by the situation.

One road sign marks direction straight to the Asian masses pressed down and exploited immemorially in the social order that contains them. To such, communism presents ominous and winning, if deceptive, appeal. The elder Masaryk observed that the Communist germ throve in sick social organisms only. Asia will scarcely be saved from the Red miasma apart from the United States sharing liberally there the West's economic resources and technical experience.

A second highway of service to the free world beckons along which America more nearly than now would become the conscience as well as the arsenal of democracy. Democracy confidently represents itself to the world as the one sufficient ideological answer to totalitarian communism. Assured of the claim's validity, we aspire to the peerage among democracies, though we know we are not a paragon either by confession or by acceptance at large. To run the race, there needs be cast off the handicaps of inefficiency, favoritism, waste and corruption in government; the power and claims of class whether of an industrial, labor or farm bloc that would subordinate public interests to its own; inequalities as between races and faiths; "sick" social levels of submarginal housing, food, and clothing; and whatsoever in state, society or community abases the dignity of the individual and infringes his birthright of freedom.

On another road, stalk ancient and hardy foes of democracy. They appear in varied guise. Their waving the American flag is not a sufficient credential. Some zealots for national safety and ideas held sacrosant would leap over the barriers of the Bill of Rights in pursuit of quarry. They are found in the halls of Congress legislating out of entry to our country men and women in flight from tyranny, whose kind once found asylum here and helped make America's most valued ideals. Their tactics undermine public confidence.

Another misconception of patriotism induces effort to blanket knowledge at the source and to seal off original inquiry and free discussion. This school of operators would condition our educational system to political, economic and social orthodoxy from the elementary schools to post-graduate universities. Erstwhile unpopular thinkers do not necessarily nor usually prove dangerous. They turn out often to be the Tom Paines and Owen Lovejoys. We are not reduced to such extremities of impotence and panic as to rush hither and yon stifling every irritating force, smothering every opposing voice while the totalitarian opponent moves inexorably in single direction and devotion to his cause.

Finally, we shall watch over the children's path. This whole generation of Americans probably will have the burden and anxiety of costly defense to carry. Their obligation may extend beyond that, even to the point of supreme sacrifice. The State, the Church, the School, the Home have the duty and the privilege under God, to convey to youth the worth of our Democracy, its meaning, its value to themselves, to the human race and the long future; its virtues and its faults to be corrected; the prices paid for its preservation and furtherance in the past, and yet to be paid. The new President has again truly declared the absorbing struggle of our time to be "one of the spirit," . . . "for the hearts and souls of men." And Karl Marx, Lenin and Stalin have not dug deeply enough to reach and contaminate the springs of American character and spirit. But they confront us with the supreme challenge of modern times.